BAYOUBLISS

LSU'S AMAZING SEASON: NATIONAL CHAMPIONS

GANNETT
LOUISIANA NEWSPAPERS

Acknowledgments
Bayou Bliss | Gannett Louisiana Newspapers

The Times
Shreveport
Pete Zanmiller, President/Publisher
Alan English, Executive Editor

The Town Talk
Alexandria
Ed Humphrey, President/Publisher
Paul Carty, Executive Editor

The Daily Advertiser
Lafayette
Leslie Hurst, President/Publisher
Denise Richter, Executive Editor

The News-Star
Monroe
David B. Petty, President/Publisher
Kathy Spurlock, Executive Editor

Daily World
Opelousas
Leslie Hurst, President/Publisher
Sebreana Domingue, Managing Editor

Book Editor
Scott Ferrell

Book Photo Editor
Mike Silva

The Photographers & Writers

Shane Bevel
The Times

Douglas Collier
The Times

Tim Eddington
Special to *The Times*

Val Horvath
The Times

Jim Hudelson
The Times

Bill Luster
Louisville Courier-Journal

Larry McCormack
The Tennessean

Pat McDonogh
Louisville Courier-Journal

Ryan Moore
The Clarion-Ledger

Greg Pearson
The Times

Mike Silva
The Times

Randy Snyder
Special to *The Times*

Sam Upshaw Jr.
Louisville Courier-Journal

Keith Warren
The Clarion-Ledger

Teddy Allen
The Times

Glenn Guilbeau
Louisiana Gannett News

Bob Heist
The Daily Advertiser

Roy Lang III
The Times

John Marcase
The Town Talk

Bob Tompkins
The Town Talk

Sanford Myers
The Tennessean

Copyright© 2008 • ISBN: 978-1-59725-128-0

Table of Contents

Foreword

By James Carville

In Louisiana, we live by the five F's – family, friends, faith, food, and most importantly football. And it just so happens that during this time of year, we get to enjoy them all together. But football is king, especially LSU football.

I grew up 17 miles downriver from Tiger Stadium in Carville, Louisiana. And I've seen hundreds of games in my 63 years. Many of the more indelible memories I have of my lifetime are marked by LSU games. From Billy Cannon's storied punt return in '59 to the Earthquake game to the 2003 championship game to the way the nation rallied around the Tigers in 2005 after Hurricanes Katrina and Rita against Arizona State. Each team has a story to tell. But this season has been special. Any one of five games from the 2007 season will have its place amongst the best LSU games of my lifetime. Each game had a different story.

From fake field goals to close calls to triple-overtime losses to coaching rumors to BCS shakeups, there's never been a college football season like this one. From start to finish, each weekend felt like a no-one-could-have-scripted-it-this-way event. And at the forefront were our LSU Tigers. Sure, they started the season ranked at the top of the polls, but no one could predict how they would finish there.

LSU opened the Division I football season in Starkville with a 45-0 rout over the much-improved Mississippi State Bulldogs. And then we had to face Virginia Tech in their first away game since the tragic mass murders on their campus in April. The 48-7 victory was perhaps the most impressive win of a long season, and one that gave the media a reason to believe that LSU was a step above the rest. After trouncing Middle Tennessee

State, the Ol' Ball Coach came to town on a rainy Saturday afternoon. Everyone will remember the fake field goal in which Matt Flynn flicked the ball over his head to speedy kicker Colt David as he dashed into the end zone for some time to come. Follow that up with a closer-than-expected victory over Tulane and then the Florida Gators came to town. Eventual Heisman winner Tim Tebow put on a clinic, but there were too many tricks (five fourth-down conversions to be exact) hidden under Les Miles' hat, and the Tigers prevailed in a nail biter. Late in the second half, I got word that USC had been upset by Stanford. I didn't believe it. And then came word over the speakers in Death Valley. It might have been just as loud of an eruption as when Eddie Fuller caught Tommy Hodson's pass late in the fourth quarter in 1988. Tiger Stadium was buzzing with national title talk.

We rode that victory on to Lexington, but were stopped by Andre Woodson and the Kentucky Wildcats in a wild triple-overtime defeat. But it was clear that there was still hope, as highly ranked teams were dropping like flies. Next up was a last-second touchdown victory over Auburn in which the Tiger faithful were asking, "What were you thinking?" as time ticked off and Flynn found Demetrius Byrd in the end zone (rather than kicking a game-winning field goal).

And then we all traveled in packs to meet former coach Nick Saban and the Alabama Crimson Tide. After a 41-34 victory, the Tigers kept plugging away with their title hopes still alive as they trounced Louisiana Tech and Ole Miss. Only Ar-Kansas stood in our way. But a funny thing happened. With stuffed stomachs, we watched Arkansas' Darren McFadden, who I consider to be the best college running back since Jim Brown, make his case for the Heisman Trophy en route to another triple overtime

defeat for the Tigers in a post-Thanksgiving classic.

So heading into Atlanta to face Tennessee, expectations were low. A roster full of injuries including starting quarterback Flynn. Rumors of Miles departing for Michigan. And an opponent who had more to prove. But none of it mattered. The Tigers made a statement that they were the best team in the SEC with their 21-14 win over the Volunteers. And then this crazy college football season got even crazier as we all huddled around television sets to watch Oklahoma manhandle Mizzou and a lowly Pittsburgh team embarrass West Virginia. I'm not a fan of the pollsters or the BCS, but we somehow squeezed through and catapulted our way back into the national championship game.

So we end the year right where we started at the top of the polls. It certainly wasn't the route expected, but it was a fun ride. After the heartbreaking Arkansas loss, someone had written on a dry erase board in the locker room, "Effort, toughness, passion — This is LSU!" And it certainly is. But LSU is also perseverance and pride. It is community and family and religion all in one. The Tigers are the heart of this state. They keep us pumping and thriving. They pick us up when we're down, and give us something to cheer for when it seems like hope is lost. LSU isn't just the school I graduated from or a championship team of football players. LSU is the spirit of the state of Louisiana. And it sure feels good to win! ■

James Carville, an LSU and LSU Law alum, became America's best-known political consultant after he helped William Jefferson Clinton win the Presidency in 1992. He is an author, actor, producer, speaker, and restaurateur. Currently, Carville is hosting XM Satellite Radio's "60/20 Sports" and is a frequent political commentator and contributor on CNN.

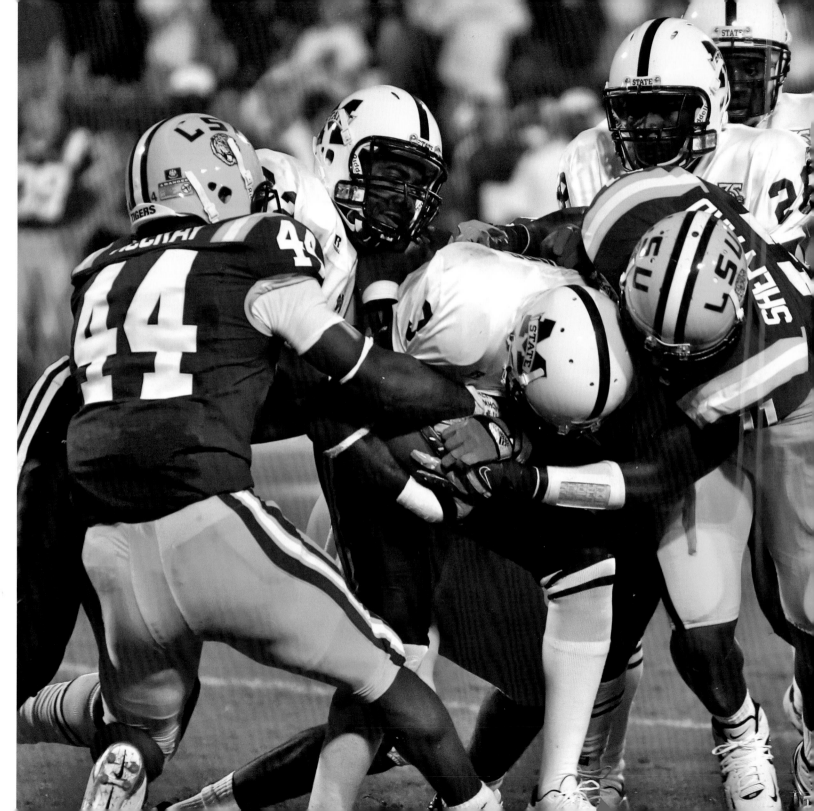

Mississippi State

Above: Mississippi State quarterback Michael Henig drops back to pass against the LSU defense. Henig was intercepted six times by the LSU defense in the game. *Photo by Ryan Moore/The Clarion-Ledger*

Left: LSU's Danny McCray (44) and Kelvin Sheppard (11) make a tackle on Mississippi State's Derek Pegues during the Tigers' 45-0 win over the Bulldogs. *Photo by Keith Warren/The Clarion-Ledger*

7

Tigers pick six in win over Mississippi State

By Glenn Guilbeau | Louisiana Gannett News

Mississippi State head football coach Sylvester Croom said he was looking forward to the 2007 season because he had a gun to hunt with rather than the switch he had for opponents in his first three seasons.

Nickel defensive back Danny McCray made the first interception at the State 45-yard line. After the drive stalled, Colt David booted a 27-yard field goal for a 3-0 LSU lead with 6:28 to go in the first quarter. Corner-back Jonathan Zenon made the second interception at the State 38. Eight plays later, Keiland Williams' 1-yard touchdown run and David extra point made it 10-0 with 5:52 to play before halftime.

He may consider a switch from the passing game altogether.

Les Miles' Tigers (1-0, 1-0 Southeastern Conference) collected six interceptions in a game for the first time since beating Tulane 42-6 in 1975. The Tigers came within two picks of the school record of eight set in 1951 in a 45-7 win over Villanova.

"I couldn't believe it," said senior strong safety Craig Steltz, who intercepted three of the passes and returned the last two 49 and 51 yards to set up touchdowns. He became the first LSU player to intercept three passes in a game since Corey Webster in 2002 and tied the school record.

"We were keeping count on the sidelines," Steltz said. "We knew how many we had. It was a great feeling to get three in one game and for the team to get six. It was an awesome feeling. To get three, you've really got to be lucky and just being in the right place at the right time."

The six interceptions by Henig tied the State school record set in 1949 by Max Stainbrock. A junior who has been starting games since 2005, Henig completed just 11 of 28 passes for 120 yards.

"I think it was obvious that it was not the best game for Mike," Croom said. "It is possible he might have been trying to make the play happen when it wasn't there."

Henig was pressured throughout the night and sacked three times.

"Any time you have Glenn Dorsey and Al Woods pressuring the quarterback like they did tonight, his eyes are as big as mine," Steltz said. "The last thing he's worried about is who's covering his people. He's just getting rid of it."

Croom probably would not mind a switch to LSU quarterback Matt Flynn, who completed 12 of 19 passes for 128 yards and two touchdowns with zero interceptions in his opening night as LSU's permanent starting quarterback after four years of waiting. He also ran on several designed plays, finishing with 42 yards on 11 carries.

"It's a dream come true," Flynn said. "It feels good. I feel very fortunate to be on a team like this. With the defense playing like it was, they made it easy for us. All I had to do was manage the game."

Flynn struggled at times, but he overcame three sacks and a near interception in the flat. LSU totaled 347 yards of offense and 22 first downs. Tailback Jacob Hester gained 68 yards on 14 carries, and Keiland Williams added 42 on 11 rushes.

Right: LSU quarterback Matt Flynn gets set to call the signals during the Tigers' 45-0 season-opening win over Mississippi State in Starkville, Miss. *Photo by Keith Warren/The Clarion-Ledger*

The defense, as expected, carried the night. State (0-1, 0-1 SEC) mustered just 10 yards rushing on 26 attempts.

"All in all, it was a great night," said LSU coach Les Miles. "It was a good start. We have to improve. Our defense gave us a lot of turnovers."

Nickel defensive back Danny McCray made the first interception at the State 45-yard line. After the drive stalled, Colt David booted a 27-yard field goal for a 3-0 LSU lead with 6:28 to go in the first quarter. Cornerback Jonathan Zenon made the second LSU interception at the State 38. Eight plays later, Williams' 1-yard touchdown run and David extra point made it 10-0 with 5:52 to play before halftime.

Free safety Curtis Taylor, who has replaced first-round draft choice LaRon Landry, ruined good field position for State at its 45 when he intercepted Henig and returned it 22 yards to State's 41. Seven plays later, Williams scored again from the 1-yard line as the final seconds of the half ticked away for a 17-0 lead.

The Tigers took a 24-0 lead with the first possession of the third quarter as Flynn took LSU 73 yards in six plays, completing all three of his passes to wide receiver Early Doucet for 34 yards, including the touchdown from 11 yards out at the 12:53 mark. Flynn also had a 21-yard scramble in the drive to the State 11. Doucet led all receivers with nine catches for 78 yards.

The fifth interception of the night and second by Steltz set LSU up at the 8-yard line after his 49-yard return. Two plays later, Flynn dropped a short pitch pass over the middle to tailback Charles Scott for an 11-yard touchdown and 31-0 lead with 2:09 to play in the third period. Steltz returned his third interception 51 yards to the State 44.

"I need to get a touchdown," Steltz said. "But every time I get one, the end zone is farther away."

Quarterback Ryan Perrilloux replaced Flynn at this point, and from the shotgun formation he scored on a 3-yard run on a draw for a 38-0 lead with 8:20 to play. Perrilloux later hit receiver Brandon LaFell on a 15-yard touchdown pass with 5:45 to play for a 38-0 lead and the first touchdown pass of Perrilloux's career. ■

Above: Mississippi State's Anthony Dixon looks for running room against the LSU defense. Dixon was held to 29 yards rushing in the game. *Photo by Keith Warren/The Clarion-Ledger*

Left: An LSU cheerleader cheers for the No. 2 Tigers in their season-opening win at Mississippi State.
Photo by Keith Warren/The Clarion-Ledger

Right: Mississippi State's Jamar Chaney tries to defend a pass to LSU's Jacob Hester (18) during LSU's 45-0 win.
Photo by Keith Warren/The Clarion-Ledger

Above: LSU's defensive front of Kirston Pittman (49), Glenn Dorsey (72), Charles Alexander (91) and Tyson Jackson (93) get ready for a play while backed by linebackers Luke Sanders (35) and Darry Beckwith (48). *Photo by Keith Warren/The Clarion-Ledger*

Left: LSU linebacker Ali Highsmith (7) makes a tackle during the Tigers' 45-0 win over Mississippi State.
Photo by Keith Warren/The Clarion-Ledger

Far left: LSU linebacker Ali Highsmith tries to bring down Missis-sippi State running back Anthony Dixon during the season-opening game in Starkville, Miss. *Photo by Keith Warren/The Clarion-Ledger*

#2 LSU vs. Mississippi State
August 30, 2007 | Starkville, MS

SCORING SUMMARY

Team	1st	2nd	3rd	4th	End
LSU	3	14	14	14	45
Miss. State	0	0	0	0	0

First quarter
LSU – Colt David 27 field goal 6:28

Second quarter
LSU – Keiland Williams 1 run (David kick) 5:52
LSU – Williams 1 run (David kick) 0:00

Third quarter
LSU – Early Doucet 11 pass from Matt Flynn (David kick) 12:53
LSU – Charles Scott 11 pass from Flynn (David kick) 2:09

Fourth quarter
LSU – Ryan Perrilloux 3 run (David kick) 8:20
LSU – Brandon LaFell 15 pass from Perrilloux (David kick) 5:45

TEAM STATS

	LSU	MSU
First Downs	22	9
Russ-Pass-Penalty	11-10-1	2-6-1
Rushes-Yards	50-198	26-10
Passing Yards	149	136
Com-Att-Int	14-22-0	14-33-6
Total Plays	72	59
Total Yards	347	146
Avg Gain Per Play	4.8	2.5
Fumbles: No.-Lost	0-0	3-1
Penalties: No.-Yards	8-60	7-39
Punts-Avg	7-44.9	5-35.6
Punt Returns: No.-Yards	1-5	4-18
Kickoff Returns: No.-Yards	1-26	7-131
Interceptions: No.-Yards	6-122	0-0
Fumble Returns: No.-Yards	0-0	0-0
Possession Time	32:45	27:15
Third-Down Conv.	6-14	3-14
Fourth-Down Conv.	0-0	0-2
Sacks By: No.-Yards	4-37	3-19

INDIVIDUAL STATS: LSU

Rushing	No.	Yds	TD	Lg
Jacob Hester	14	68	0	17
Matt Flynn	11	42	0	21
Richard Murphy	6	35	0	21
Trindon Holliday	6	19	0	11
Keiland Williams	7	18	2	13
Ryan Perrilloux	3	12	1	8
Charles Scott	3	4	0	5

Passing	Att	Cmp	Int	Yds	TD	Lg
Matt Flynn	19	12	0	128	2	19
Ryan Perrilloux	3	2	0	21	1	15

Receiving	No.	Yds	TD	Lg
Early Doucet	9	78	1	18
Terrance Toliver	1	19	0	19
Chris Mitchell	1	16	0	16
Brandon LaFell	1	15	1	15
Charles Scott	1	11	1	11
Jacob Hester	1	10	0	10

Punting	No.	Yds	Avg	Lg
Patrick Fisher	7	314	44.9	56

INDIVIDUAL STATS: Mississippi State

Rushing	No.	Yds	TD	Lg
Anthony Dixon	13	29	0	10
Justin Williams	4	10	0	4
Christian Ducre	1	2	0	2
Wesley Carroll	3	-6	0	2
Michael Henig	4	-22	0	8

Passing	Att	Cmp	Int	Yds	TD	Lg
Michael Henig	28	11	6	120	0	45
Wesley Carroll	5	3	0	16	0	12

Receiving	No.	Yds	TD	Lg
Arnil Stallworth	3	33	0	20
Lance Long	2	16	0	12
Christian Ducre	2	2	0	3
Tony Burks	1	45	0	45
Jason Husband	1	26	0	26
Jamayel Smith	1	11	0	11
Justin Williams	1	4	0	4
Co-Eric Riley	1	0	0	0
Jeremy Jones	1	0	0	0
Eric Butler	1	-1	0	0

Punting	No.	Yds	Avg	Lg
Blake McAdams	5	178	35.6	44

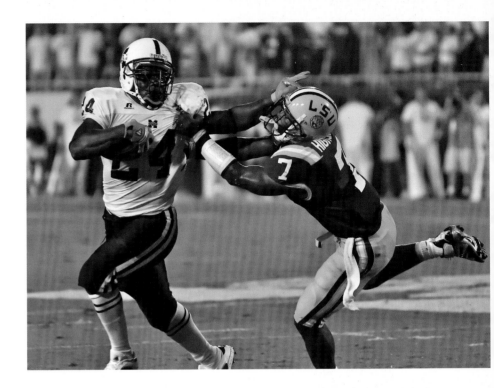

Above: Mississippi State quarterback Michael Henig (7) begins a play during his team's 45-0 loss to LSU in Starkville, Miss. *Photo by Keith Warren/The Clarion-Ledger*

Left: LSU wide receiver Early Doucet (9) hauls in a pass during his team's season-opening victory at Mississippi State. *Photo by Keith Warren/The Clarion-Ledger*

Opposite top: Mississippi State running back Anthony Dixon (24) tries to elude LSU linebacker Ali Highsmith (7) during the team's game in Starkville, Miss. *Photo by Keith Warren/The Clarion-Ledger*

Opposite bottom: LSU quarterback Matt Flynn (15) changes the play at the line of scrimmage during the Tigers' season-opening win over Mississippi State. *Photo by Keith Warren/The Clarion-Ledger*

Virginia Tech

GAME TWO 9.8.07 ■ VIRGINIA TECH **7** | LSU **48**

Above: LSU head coach Les Miles gestures to the crowd as he and the LSU Tigers make their way to Tiger Stadium to take on Virginia Tech. *Photo by Douglas Collier/The Times*

Left: Fans cheers their LSU Tigers as they take the field to warm up. *Photo by Douglas Collier/The Times*

Tigers hammer Hokies in top-10 battle

By Glenn Guilbeau | Louisiana Gannett News

It's starting to look a lot like New Year's in New Orleans.

Second-ranked LSU made a large bid for the nation's No. 1 ranking with a hellacious Hokie throwdown, beating No. 9 Virginia Tech into submission, 48-7, in front of 92,739 — the largest crowd in Tiger Stadium history.

It was LSU's most lopsided victory ever over an Associated Press top-10 team. It was Virginia Tech's most lopsided loss since a 45-0 fallout at Vanderbilt in 1982.

The Tigers (2-0) went into the game far behind No. 1 and idle USC (1-0) in individual voting in both the Associated Press media poll and the USA Today coaches poll. The BCS national championship game will be at the Superdome in New Orleans on Jan. 7.

"I'm not sure they're not the No. 1 team in the country," said Virginia Tech coach Frank Beamer after the worst beating of his coaching career, which started in 1987 at the Blacksburg, Va., school. "They really took it to us. They didn't make mistakes. They didn't turn the ball over. They hit us."

ESPN.com senior writer Pat Forde covered the game.

"I'd put them No. 1," he said. "Based on what I've seen, they should be No. 1."

LSU had amassed 448 yards after just three quarters. By game's merciful end, LSU had 598 yards to 149 by Tech. The Tigers outrushed the Hokies 297 yards to 71 and had 28 first downs to 11.

The most yardage Tech allowed last season was 344 to Wake Forest as it finished No. 1 in the nation in total defense, passing defense and scoring defense.

LSU treated Tech like a common directional non-

conference opponent instead of the traditional national power it is with five 10-win or more seasons this decade and a national championship runner-up finish in the Jan. 4, 2000 Sugar Bowl.

"We've got a lot of football left to play," LSU coach Les Miles said. "We've accomplished to a point. We have to play like that week in and week out. We have weeks to go before we can even start thinking about that."

The Tigers took a 14-0 lead in the first quarter against the Hokies just like they did last season against Louisiana-Lafayette, Tulane, Kentucky and Fresno State and breezed to an easy victory just like in those games.

Tech netted but 11 yards on nine plays in the first quarter to 207 in 25 plays by LSU and by halftime was down 24-0 on the scoreboard and 327-40 in yards. It marked the first time in two years the Hokies were held scoreless in a first half.

LSU tailback Keiland Williams led all rushers with 126 yards on seven carries and scored on runs of 67 and 32 yards. Quarterback Matt Flynn completed 17 of 27 passes for 217 yards, and backup Ryan Perrilloux hit 5 of 5 passes for 84 yards and a pair of touchdowns.

On LSU's second play from scrimmage, tailback Jacob Hester blew up Tech's vaunted defense with a 13-yard run up the gut. Flynn shovel passed to Hester for a 28-yard gain to the 3-yard line, where Hester scored a play later to cap a 10-play, 87-yard drive that resembled a drill. It was 7-0 just over four minutes into the game. Hester finished with 81 yards on 12 carries. Trindon Holliday gained another 36 on four carries.

"We put some rushing yardage on a very, very talented defense," Miles said. "I can tell you, there were some holes. We ran some power plays right at them.

Our defense played extremely well. Guys wearing our helmets were all around the football."

On Tech's first third down of the game, free safety Curtis Taylor sacked Tech quarterback Sean Glennon for a 6-yard loss. A punt and a play later, Flynn found wide receiver Brandon LaFell on a slant for 56 yards to the Tech 25. Six plays later, Flynn picked his way behind blockers for a 7-yard touchdown, and it was 14-0 with 5:54 to go in the first period.

Glennon finished the first quarter 1-of-5 passing with an interception by strong safety Craig Steltz that set up a 30-yard field goal by Colt David for a 17-0 lead early in the second quarter.

LSU went up 24-0 with 11:55 to go in the second quarter on a 67-yard touchdown run by Williams. It was the longest touchdown run from scrimmage by LSU since Alley Broussard's 74 yarder in the Capital One Bowl on Jan. 1, 2005. ■

Top: LSU's Jacob Hester is stopped by Virginia Tech's Xavier Adibi during the Tigers' 48-7 win over the Hokies in Tiger Stadium. *Photo by Douglas Collier/The Times*

Bottom: LSU's Jacob Hester breaks through the Virginia Tech defense during the Tigers' game against the Hokies in Baton Rouge. *Photo by Douglas Collier/The Times*

Opposite top: Matt Flynn takes the snap during the LSU Tigers' game against the Virginia Tech Hokies. LSU won 48-7. *Photo by Douglas Collier/The Times*

Opposite bottom: The LSU cheerleaders show their spirit in the home opener against Virginia Tech. *Photo by Douglas Collier/The Times*

Top: Fans cheer on the LSU Tigers as they warm up before their game against Virginia Tech.
Photo by Douglas Collier/The Times

Above: Tiger Stadium erupts as the LSU Tigers take the field during pregame warm-ups.
Photo by Douglas Collier/The Times

Opposite: Trindon Holliday runs for yardage. *Photo by Douglas Collier/The Times*

#9 Virginia Tech vs. #2 LSU
September 8, 2007 | Baton Rouge, LA

SCORING SUMMARY

Team	1st	2nd	3rd	4th	End
Virginia Tech	0	0	7	0	7
LSU	14	10	10	14	48

First quarter
LSU – Jacob Hester 3 run (Colt David kick) 10:46
LSU – Matt Flynn 7 run (David kick) 5:54

Second quarter
LSU – David 30 field goal 14:55
LSU – Keiland Williams 67 run (David kick) 11:55

Third quarter
LSU – David 28 field goal 8:30
VT – Tyrod Taylor 1 run (Jud Dunlevy) 4:38
LSU – Early Doucet 34 pass from Ryan Perrilloux (David kick) 1:36

Fourth quarter
LSU – Williams 32 run (David kick) 9:29
LSU – Terrance Toliver 28 pass from Perrilloux (David kick) 3:18

TEAM STATS

	VT	LSU
First Downs	11	28
Rush-Pass-Penalty	4-4-3	10-15-3
Rushes-Yards	28-71	41-297
Passing Yards	78	301
Com-Att-Int	9-29-1	22-32-0
Total Plays	57	73
Total Yards	149	598
Avg. Gain Per Play	2.6	8.2
Fumbles: No.-Lost	1-0	0-0
Penalties: No.-Yards	7-65	7-62
Punts-Avg.	8-40.1	3-44.7
Kickoff Returns: No.-Yards	2-124	9-57.1
Interceptions: No.-Yards	0-0	1-11
Fumble Returns: No.-Yards	0-0	0-0
Possession Time	25:27	34:33
Third-Down Conv.	2-14	9-15
Fourth-Down Conv.	1-2	0-0
Sacks By: No.-Yards	2-2	3-22

INDIVIDUAL STATISTICS: Virginia Tech

Rushing	No	Yds	TD	Lg
Tyrod Taylor	9	44	1	23
Branden Ore	14	28	0	9
Sean Glennon	2	2	0	8
Kenny Lewis	1	1	0	1
Carlton Weatherford	1	0	0	0
Eddie Royal	1	-4	0	0

Passing	Att	Com	Int	Yds	TD	Lg
Tyrod Taylor	18	7	0	62	0	19
Sean Glennon	10	2	1	16	0	11
Eddie Royal	1	0	0	0	0	0

Receiving	No	Yds	TD	Lg
Josh Morgan	4	20	0	13
Branden Ore	2	24	0	19
Chris Drager	1	14	0	14
Justin Harper	1	11	0	11
Ike Whitaker	1	9	0	19

Punting	No.	Yds	Avg	Lg
Brent Bowden	8	321	40.1	44

INDIVIDUAL STATISTICS: LSU

Rushing	No	Yds	TD	Lg
Keiland Williams	7	126	2	67
Jacob Hester	12	81	1	21
Trindon Holliday	4	32	0	22
Charles Scott	4	24	0	14
Ryan Perrilloux	4	21	0	9
Matt Flynn	7	12	1	7
Richard Murphy	2	2	0	1

Passing	Att	Com	Int	Yds	TD	Lg
Matt Flynn	27	17	0	217	0	56
Ryan Perrilloux	5	5	0	84	2	34

Receiving	No	Yds	TD	Lg
Brandon LaFell	7	125	0	56
Early Doucet	6	75	1	34
Demetrius Byrd	2	22	0	12
Keiland Williams	2	10	0	6
Jacob Hester	1	28	0	28
Terrance Toliver	1	28	0	28
Charles Scott	1	11	0	11
Trindon Holliday	1	3	0	3
Jared Mitchell	1	-1	0	0

Punting	No.	Yds	Avg	Lg
Patrick Fisher	3	134	44.7	61

Left: Les Miles talks with running back Richard Murphy. *Photo by Douglas Collier/The Times*

Right: The team celebrates a touchdown. *Photo by Douglas Collier/The Times*

Right middle: Jacob Hester runs for a big gain. *Photo by Douglas Collier/The Times*

Right bottom: Lazarius Levingston after a sack. *Photo by Douglas Collier/The Times*

Below: Matt Flynn calls out a play. *Photo by Douglas Collier/The Times*

Opposite: Keiland Williams prays. *Photo by Douglas Collier/The Times*

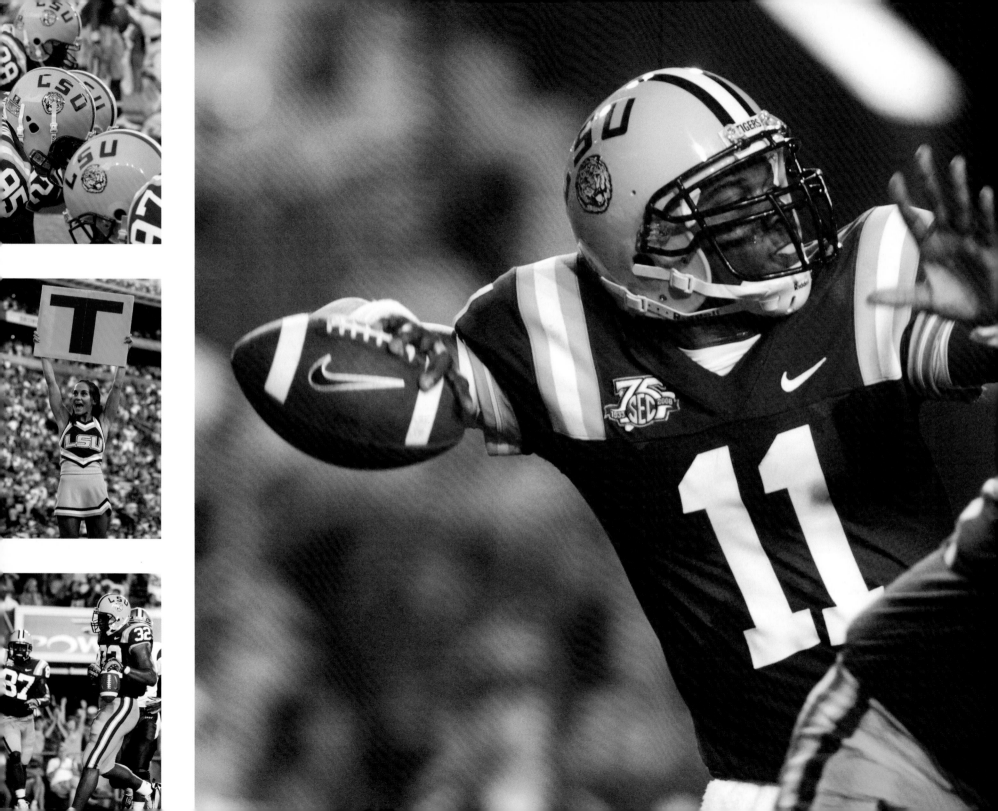

Middle Tennessee

GAME THREE 9.15.07 ■ MIDDLE TENNESSEE **0** | LSU **44**

Above: The LSU band performs on the field before the start of the game against MTSU.
Photo by Shane Bevel/The Times

Left: LSU's Ryan Perrilloux pulls the trigger on a 63-yard touchdown pass under protection from Carnell Stewart during the first half of the game against MTSU in Baton Rouge. *Photo by Shane Bevel/The Times*

Backups lead blowout of Middle Tennessee

By Glenn Guilbeau | Louisiana Gannett News

He hasn't won the Heisman yet, but quarterback Ryan Perrilloux showed he was the man at least for one night.

The oft-troubled super signee from East St. John High in LaPlace made Tiger Stadium his place as he replaced injured Matt Flynn and threw for 298 yards and three touchdowns to lead No. 2 LSU over Middle Tennessee, 44-0, in front of 92,407.

"It was a great feeling to go out there in front of the whole crowd," said Perrilloux, who completed 20 of 25 passes, including 6 of 6 in the third quarter, which was his last.

"I just wanted to go out there, be calm, play within the system and good things will happen."

Flynn, who suffered an ankle injury against Virginia Tech, dressed out. LSU coach Les Miles said he could have played if needed and expects him to play next week in the Southeastern Conference opener next week against South Carolina. Flynn was available for emergency use, but 9-1-1 was never needed.

Perrilloux threw lasers. He threw deep.

He threw a 62-yard touchdown pass to wide receiver Demetrius Byrd that went nearly 50 yards in the air for a 17-0 lead in the second quarter. He scrambled for 37 yards.

He held on field goals and extra points. He even blocked on a reverse pitch to Brandon LaFell for an 18-yard touchdown and 30-0 lead midway in the third quarter. There was just one interception.

"He throws a 99 mile an hour fastball," Byrd said. "He really throws the ball hard, but he has great accu-

racy. He's a great quarterback. Great arm."

Perrilloux came out firing. After missing on his first two passes as LSU was held to a 29-yard field goal on its first possession, Perrilloux found Byrd for a 24-yard gain. He gained eight yards on a run. He hit tight end Richard Dickson for 10 yards, then wide receiver Jared Mitchell for another 10 and then threw a 13-yard touchdown to tailback Charles Scott for a 10-0 lead on the last play of the first quarter.

After throwing an interception right to Middle Tennessee safety Dana Stewart, Perrilloux didn't hesitate and threw the bomb to Byrd for the touchdown.

"He tried to hit the linebacker (actually a safety) not only in the chest but in between the ribs," Miles said. "But he handled the pressure in the pocket. He got roughed up (two sacks). Still, he came back and seemed to have composure and played well."

This was always how it was supposed to be when Perrilloux reneged on a commitment to Texas and signed with LSU and Miles in February of 2005 in an otherwise lackluster class. On signing day, he announced he would win the Heisman Trophy in his first season. Nevermind that JaMarcus Russell and Flynn had a healthy lead on him on the depth chart. He was redshirted that season, then completed just 1 of 4 passes in 2006 as the No. 3 quarterback. After missing meetings and weight lifting sessions, Perrilloux was not in good favor with Miles throughout his first two years and was suspended last spring after receiving a citation from Baton Rouge Police for using fake identification at a local gambling casino.

Miles lifted the suspension as practices began in August but listed Perrilloux as his No. 3 quarterback. Perrilloux kept his nose clean and moved up the depth

chart. He played briefly in LSU's first two games, but he completed 7 of 8 passes for 105 yards and three touchdowns.

"It was a good thing I stayed and stuck it out," Perrilloux said. "Every player doubts himself sometimes, but you just have to keep pushing forward. The coaches know what they're doing."

After LaFell's touchdown, Perrilloux threw a perfect 15-yard strike over the middle to wide receiver Terrance Toliver in the back of the end zone for a 37-0 lead midway in the third quarter. Perrilloux completed all three of his passes for 60 yards on LSU's next possession, setting up an 8-yard touchdown run by tailback Richard Murphy for the 44-0 lead with 1:28 to play in the third period.

Perrilloux sat out the fourth quarter as another backup — Harvard transfer Andrew Hatch — finished the game. LSU put up 505 yards of total offense without star receiver Early Doucet, who injured himself Friday and did not dress out. LSU (3-0) held the Blue Raiders (0-3) to 90 yards of offense.

Miles informed Perrilloux on Saturday afternoon that he would be starting for sure, though Perrilloux had a good idea all week since he got most of the work. And it showed.

"He hit 20 of 25 passes and threw for 300 yards," Miles said. "That's not a bad day at the office." ■

Opposite top: An LSU cheerleader revs up the crowd at Tiger Stadium for the game against MTSU in Baton Rouge.
Photo by Shane Bevel/The Times

Opposite bottom: The LSU cheerleaders run the flags after a touchdown in the first half of the game against MTSU.
Photo by Shane Bevel/The Times

Right: The Tigers line up in pregame drills before the game against MTSU at Tiger Stadium. *Photo by Shane Bevel/The Times*

Middle Tennessee vs. #2 LSU
September 15, 2007 | Baton Rouge, LA

SCORING SUMMARY

Team	1st	2nd	3rd	4th	End
Middle Tennessee	0	0	0	0	0
LSU	10	13	21	0	44

First quarter
LSU – Colt David 29 field goal 10:36
LSU – Charles Scott 13 pass from Ryan Perrilloux (David kick) 0:00
Second quarter
LSU – Demetrius Byrd 62 pass from Perrilloux (David kick) 9:47
LSU – David 35 field goal 3:04
LSU – David 26 field goal 0:00
Third quarter
LSU – Brandon LaFell 18 run (David kick) 9:07
LSU – Terrance Toliver 15 pass from Perrilloux (David kick) 8:01
LSU – Richard Murphy 8 run (David kick) 1:28

TEAM STATS

	MTSU	LSU
First Downs	9	26
Rush-Pass-Penalty	5-3-1	12-14-0
Rushes-Yards	37-9	40-198
Passing Yards	81	307
Comp-Att-Int	8-15-0	21-28-1
Total Plays	52	68
Total Yards	90	505
Avg. Gain Per Play	1.7	7.4
Fumbles No.-Lost	1-1	2-1
Penalties No.-Yards	3-20	10-58
Punts-Avg.	8-37.4	1-41.0
Punt Returns No.-Yds	0-0	2-10
Kickoff Returns No.-Yds	7-119	1-24
Interceptions: No.-Yds	1-18	0-0
Fumble Returns No.-Yds	0-0	0-0
Possession Time	31:09	28:51
Third Down Conv.	4-14	8-12
Fourth Down Conv.	0-2	0-0
Sacks By: No.-Yds	2-15	6-58

INDIVIDUAL STATS: Middle Tennessee

Rushing	No.	Yds	TD	Lg
Dwight Dasher	12	30	0	12
DeMarco McNair	8	8	0	6
Phillip Tanner	6	2	0	2
M. Branton	2	0	0	2
Desmond Gee	2	-1	0	3
Joe Craddock	7	-30	0	5

INDIVIDUAL STATS: Middle Tennessee

Passing	Att	Cmp	Int	Yds	TD	Lg
Joe Craddock	11	6	0	59	0	14
Dwight Dasher	4	2	0	22	0	19

Receiving	No.	Yds	TD	Lg
DeMarco McNair	2	25	0	14
P. Honeycutt	2	21	0	12
Wes Caldwell	1	19	0	19
Phillip Tanner	1	8	0	8
M. Cannon	1	5	0	5
Bobby Williams	1	3	0	3

Punting	No.	Yds	Avg	Lg
David DeFatta	8	299	37.4	52

INDIVIDUAL STATS: LSU

Rushing	No.	Yds	TD	Lg
Jacob Hester	10	57	0	22
Ryan Perrilloux	8	37	0	16
Keiland Williams	5	30	0	11
Andrew Hatch	4	27	0	11
Brandon LaFell	1	18	1	18
Charles Scott	3	17	0	7
Richard Murphy	3	15	1	8
Trindon Holliday	3	4	0	5

Passing	Att	Cmp	Int	Yds	TD	Lg
Ryan Perrilloux	25	20	1	298	3	62
Andrew Hatch	2	1	0	9	0	9

Receiving	No.	Yds.	TD	Lg
Jared Mitchell	6	82	0	32
Brandon LaFell	3	47	0	19
Charles Scott	3	22	1	13
Demetrius Byrd	2	86	1	62
Richard Dickson	2	20	0	10
Terrance Toliver	1	15	1	15
Keiland Williams	1	14	0	14
Ricky Dixon	1	9	0	9
Keith Zinger	1	6	0	6
Jacob Hester	1	6	0	6
Totals	21	307	3	62

Punting	No.	Yds	Avg	Lg
Patrick Fisher	1	41	41.0	41

Above: LSU's Jared Mitchell celebrates the Tigers' first touchdown, a short run by Charles Scott in the first half of the game against MTSU. *Photo by Shane Bevel/The Times*

Left: LSU linebacker Ali Highsmith drags down MTSU running back DeMarco McNair during the first half of the game at Tiger Stadium in Baton Rouge. *Photo by Shane Bevel/The Times*

Above: LSU defensive end Tyson Jackson chases down MTSU quarterback Joe Craddock in the first half of the game at Tiger Stadium. *Photo by Shane Bevel/The Times*

Right: LSU defensive tackle Glenn Dorsey hunts down MTSU quarterback Joe Craddock during the first half of the game at Tiger Stadium. *Photo by Shane Bevel/The Times*

Far right: The LSU Tiger pause for a prayer after defeating MTSU on the field at Tiger Stadium. *Photo by Shane Bevel/The Times*

Right: LSU head coach Les Miles celebrates a victory over MTSU with his Tigers on the field. *Photo by Shane Bevel/The Times*

Far right: LSU wide receiver Jared Mitchell dances along the sideline dragging a MTSU defender late in the game in front of a packed house at Tiger Stadium. *Photo by Shane Bevel/The Times*

Below: The LSU team huddles up against the backdrop of a packed Tiger Stadium at the start of the game against MTSU. *Photo by Shane Bevel/The Times*

South Carolina

GAME FOUR 9.22.07 ■ SOUTH CAROLINA **16** | LSU **28**

Above: LSU fans cheer on the Tigers in their win over South Carolina. *Photo by Val Horvath/The Times*

Left: LSU quarterback Matt Flynn (15) drops back in the pocket surrounded by guard Lyle Hitt (65) and center Brett Helms (74). *Photo by Val Horvath/The Times*

Tigers turn the table on South Carolina

By Glenn Guilbeau | Louisiana Gannett News

Steve Spurrier got beat at his own, old game.

Trick plays, misdirection, quick strikes, many plays, faster players, alternating quarterbacks and swagger — Spurrier didn't direct it this time. He had to watch No. 2 LSU do it, and it beat his No. 12 South Carolina team, 28-16, in front of 92,530 on a wet day at Tiger Stadium.

When LSU went up 21-7 late in the second quarter on a fake field goal featuring a no-look flip by holder Matt Flynn to kicker Colt David for a 15-yard touchdown, Spurrier winced on the sidelines and gritted his teeth. But his expression seemed to approve.

"It was the perfect call," Spurrier said with admiration after the game. "They got me. Obviously, when they work, they're a good call. But they executed it perfectly. Give those guys credit for that."

Then Spurrier got himself. He made a Superior blunder by going for it on fourth-and-1 from his 30-yard line midway in the third quarter against the nation's No. 1 defense, and the next thing he knew it was 28-7.

Outside linebacker Luke Sanders shot the line gap and hit tailback Cory Boyd first with defensive end Kirston Pittman following through to hold Boyd to no gain for the second consecutive play.

"If he'd have made it, it would've been a great call," said LSU coach Les Miles, who sparred playfully with Spurrier during the week. "But he didn't."

LSU took over on the Gamecocks' 30. Tailback Jacob Hester gained 24 yards on four carries, busting through a nice hole over right guard for the 9-yard scoring run and three-touchdown cushion with 6:02 to play in the third period.

"I wasn't surprised at all," Pittman said. "When you're facing Steve Spurrier, you know he's a real gutsy coach. Luke just shot the gap and really anticipated it when the tackle moved. I came over the top. It was just a great defensive play. They were gaining some momentum after just stopping our offense."

South Carolina, which led 7-0 in the first quarter and managed to keep the score down in the early going, was never in the game again after that fourth down.

"I thought at that time it was important for our offense to stay on the field and make something happen," Spurrier said. "That was their lone touchdown of the second half."

The decision came back to haunt the six-time SEC champion coach as LSU proceeded to punt on three of its next four possessions with an interception by struggling quarterback Matt Flynn in between.

The Gamecocks (3-1, 1-1 SEC) took a 23-yard field goal after driving 56 yards, cutting the lead to 28-10 midway in the fourth quarter. After a Fisher punt, South Carolina went 80 yards in 10 plays to cut it to 28-16 on a 1-yard pass from backup quarterback Chris Smelley to Kenny McKinley with 1:41 to go. LSU ran out the clock to end it.

LSU outgained South Carolina 273 yards to 89 in the first half but led only 14-7 with under four minutes to play in the second quarter. This is when LSU nickel back Danny McCray intercepted a twice-tipped pass from starting quarterback Blake Mitchell at the Gamecocks' 32-yard line.

Then LSU's line pulled a funky shift with mini back Trindon Holliday lining up right behind the left guard. Quarterback Ryan Perrilloux, who alternated by play with Flynn at times, quickly handed it to Holliday for 11 yards. The drive stalled and LSU lined up for a 32-yard

field goal with just over a minute to play in the half.

"Roxy" was called. Flynn took the snap and with head down, flipped it over his right shoulder to David, who scampered around right end untouched for the touchdown and 21-7 lead as the crowd went wild.

"I went out there to find somebody to block, and there was nobody," said Hester, who lined up at the end on the right side.

"Once I caught it, I looked up and it was wide open," David said. "I just didn't want to slip. It always works in practice, and Matt never even looks back. It's beautiful."

LSU went up 14-7 early in the second quarter on a 56-yard drive in nine plays and almost as many substitutions. Flynn opened the drive at quarterback, but Perrilloux rotated in and out and rambled 19 yards on a keeper to set up a 1-yard touchdown pass by Flynn to tight end Richard Dickson. Five players ran the ball on the drive in all.

After South Carolina drove 67 yards for a 7-0 advantage with 2:46 to play in the first quarter, the Tigers looked like Spurrier's old Florida team in tying it 7-7. They went 69 yards in just four plays and 83 seconds. Flynn, who struggled to an 8-of-19 night, found Dickson for 24 yards. Holliday took it from there, gaining 11 and then went untouched for a 33-yard touchdown with 1:16 to play in the opening period.

"I like the direction of the offense," Miles said. "It keeps a lot of people involved. I enjoyed ol' Holliday. I enjoy the fact that we're calling a lot of guys' numbers."

And that includes Colt David on the "Roxy," or what some called the "Spurrier Special," but not Miles.

"I'm not built to say that I looked to beat him," Miles said. "That's not the issue." ■

Left: LSU's Jacob Hester runs with the ball during a game against South Carolina at Tiger Stadium in Baton Rouge.

Photo by Val Horvath/The Times

Opposite: LSU quarterback Matt Flynn, left, looks to hand the ball to a teammate during a game against South Carolina.

Photo by Val Horvath/The Times

Left & below: LSU's Colt David catches a toss from quarterback Matt Flynn during a fake field goal attempt that led to a touchdown during a game against South Carolina at Tiger Stadium in Baton Rouge.

Photos by Val Horvath/The Times

LSU's trickery gets Spurrier's approval

By Roy Lang III | The Times

Matt Flynn's most successful pass went backward and Steve Spurrier admitted he was out-shenaniganed.

The LSU-South Carolina game wasn't that absurd, but one momentum-grabbing (and perhaps game-deciding) play transformed Tiger Stadium, at least briefly, into a sandlot.

"It worked perfectly," Spurrier said following his Gamecocks' 28-16 defeat that included LSU kicker Colt David's 15-yard touchdown run off a nifty pitch from a fake field goal. "They got me."

Flynn never saw his receiver (considering the rest of his day, maybe it was a good thing) or the catch and the trickery won't show up in his passing stats. But unlike a majority of the other balls he threw against South Carolina, the toss hit an intended receiver in stride, put points on the board and sent those dressed in purple in gold into a tizzy — in a good way.

Flynn's no-look over-the-head pitch to David would have made the Harlem Globetrotters proud. And there's a good bet the Ol' Ball Coach — give him time — will even chuckle about the draw-it-in-the-dirt dipsy doodle.

"Roxy" was called as the No. 2 Tigers held a tenuous seven-point advantage over the No. 12 Gamecocks late in the first half. The play the Tigers work on every day went off without a hitch and the SEC clash fell firmly in LSU's hands.

"I was worried about my footing," said David, who was alerted to the "Alert Roxy" warning as he headed onto the field.

The defensive alignment had the Tigers licking their chops and Flynn put Roxy into motion.

David took Flynn's precise toss and scampered — and don't dare say kickers can't scamper any longer — 15 yards along the rain-soaked natural surface into the end zone to give LSU a 21-7 lead with 1:10 left before halftime.

LSU head coach Les Miles called his newfound weapon, the 5-foot-7, 173-pound Grapevine, Texas, product "very fast."

The touchdown was the first of any kind, at any level, in David's career. In fact, it was the first time David was part of a fake field goal.

"He's an old soccer guy and we wondered if he could catch balls," said Miles, who believes the Tigers created

Right: LSU fans packed Tiger Stadium to watch the Tigers take on South Carolina.
Photo by Val Horvath/The Times

Below: LSU's Johnathan Zenon tries to get the crowd to make some noise during a game against South Carolina at Tiger Stadium in Baton Rouge.
Photo by Val Horvath/The Times

the play last year. "He certainly can."

South Carolina gamely hung around with the mighty Tigers, but David's dagger sent the Gamecocks to the locker room scratching their heads.

"I think it broke their spirit. It should have," David said.

South Carolina never threatened again.

"I was sitting over there wanting to go safe field goal defense because the guy just missed a 30-yarder (actually a 42-yarder)," Spurrier said. "I said, 'What are we doing here?' and somebody said, 'We're going after him.' I said, 'Well, OK.'"

South Carolina cornerback Captain Munnerlyn rushed in from the right side of LSU's protection and David had nothing but green, but wet, grass in front of him before the goal line.

David said the play — even on Flynn's end — never misfires in practice. However, the slick surface put some doubt into his mind due to the fact he, like most kickers, has shaved cleats.

"I didn't want to ruin it from the start," said David, who admitted to having butterflies when the play was called, but said the ensuing extra point was more nerve-wracking because of a racing heartbeat. "I saw the yellow (end zone) and said, 'Wow, I'm going to do this.'"

The only regret for David? The lack of a fancy celebration. This is likely the only point where the fact he's a kicker hindered him.

"I wish I would have done something," David said. "It was my first one, so I really didn't know what to do."

David's career rushing average stands at 15 yards per carry and he scores on 100 percent of the time he gets the ball into his hands. Does he expect his touches to increase?

"It would be nice," David said. ∎

Opposite top: South Carolina's Kenny McKinley, left, tries to keep away from LSU's Johnathan Zenon.
Photo by Val Horvath/The Times

Opposite middle: LSU coach Les Miles talks to referees during the South Carolina game.
Photo by Val Horvath/The Times

Opposite bottom: South Carolina's Mike Davis is chased by some LSU players.
Photo by Val Horvath/The Times

Below: The LSU band plays during the game against South Carolina at Tiger Stadium.
Photo by Val Horvath/The Times

#12 South Carolina vs #2 LSU
September 22, 2007 | Baton Rouge, LA

SCORING SUMMARY

Team	1st	2nd	3rd	4th	End
South Carolina	7	0	0	9	16
LSU	7	14	7	0	28

First quarter
USC – Mike Davis 1 run (Ryan Succop kick) 2:46
LSU – Trindon Holliday 33 run (Colt David kick) 1:16

Second quarter
LSU – Richard Dickson 1 pass from Matt Flynn (David kick) 12:13
LSU – Colt David 15 run (David kick) 1:10

Third quarter
LSU – Jacob Hester 9 run (David kick) 6:02

Fourth quarter
USC – Succop 23 field goal 7:44
USC – Kenny McKinley 1 pass from Chris Smelley (Pass failed)

TEAM STATS

	USC	LSU
First Downs	16	19
Rush-Pass-Penalty	1-13-2	16-3-0
Rushes-Yards	27-17	50-290
Passing Yards	244	70
Com-Att-Int	19-42-2	8-20-1
Total Plays	69	70
Total Yards	261	360
Avg. Gain Per Play	3.8	5.1
Fumbles: No.-Lost	2-1	3-0
Penalties: No.-Yards	2-20	5-39
Punts-Avg.	5-44.8	7-38.1
Punt Returns: No.-Yards	1-19	2-9
Kickoff Returns: No.-Yards	5-122	3-50
Interceptions: No.-Yards	1-0	2-0
Fumble Returns: No.-Yards	0-0	0-0
Possession Time	27:09	32:51
Third-Down Conv.	8-16	4-14
Fourth-Down Conv.	0-2	1-1
Sacks By: No.-Yards	1-6	3-26

INDIVIDUAL STATS: South Carolina

Rushing	No.	Yds	TD	Lg
Cory Boyd	18	17	0	6
Kenny McKinley	2	16	0	7
Mike Davis	4	10	1	5
Chris Smelley	1	-7	0	0
Blake Mitchell	2	-19	0	0

INDIVIDUAL STATS: South Carolina

Passing	Att	Cmp	Int	Yds	TD	Lg
Chris Smelley	26	12	1	174	1	45
Blake Mitchell	16	7	1	70	0	21

Receiving	No.	Yds	TD	Lg
Kenny McKinley	6	25	1	8
Cory Boyd	4	66	0	24
Weslye Saunders	4	32	0	11
Mike Davis	3	77	0	45
Moe Brown	1	27	0	27
Jared Cook	1	17	0	17

Punting	No.	Yds	Avg	Lg
Ryan Succop	5	224	44.8	50

INDIVIDUAL STATS: LSU

Rushing	No.	Yds	TD	Lg
Jacob Hester	17	88	1	15
Trindon Holliday	6	73	1	33
Ryan Perrilloux	8	59	0	23
Keiland Williams	7	33	0	14
Colt David	1	15	1	15
Richard Murphy	3	15	0	22
Charles Scott	1	7	0	7
Matt Flynn	4	6	0	5

Passing	Att	Cmp	Int	Yds	TD	Lg
Matt Flynn	19	8	1	70	1	24
Ryan Perrilloux	1	0	0	0	0	0

Receiving	No.	Yds	TD	Lg
Richard Dickson	4	39	1	24
Brandon LaFell	2	16	0	10
Quinn Johnson	1	9	0	9
Jared Mitchell	1	6	0	6

Punting	No.	Yds	Avg.	Lg
Patrick Fisher	6	245	40.8	51

Tulane

GAME FIVE 9.29.07 ■ LSU **34** | TULANE **9**

Above: LSU coach Les Miles and defensive tackle Glenn Dorsey embrace following the Tigers' 34-9 win over Tulane. *Photo by Alex Brandon/AP*

Left: LSU running back Charles Scott (32) races away from the Tulane defense. *Photo by Alex Brandon/AP*

LSU pulls away from Tulane in second half

By Glenn Guilbeau | Louisiana Gannett News

LSU overslept Saturday morning, while Tulane roared on what looked like a caffeine high.

The second-ranked Tigers eventually woke up from an 11 a.m. kickoff and nightmarish first half in which they trailed 9-7 at one point. Then 40-point underdog Tulane crashed as LSU (5-0) escaped with a 34-9 win in front of 58,769 at the Louisiana Superdome.

"If you want to say we were flat, that's it," said LSU coach Les Miles, whose team allowed four sacks in the first half and led only 10-9 at the break. "Yeah, it wasn't our best game. We played like we didn't have intent or purpose."

Tulane, which struggled to beat Division I-AA Southeastern Louisiana 35-27 a week ago and came in as the largest underdog in the history of this once-searing state rivalry, played on fire.

The Green Wave (1-3) sacked LSU quarterback Matt Flynn four times in the first half and forced a hold from a sluggish offensive line for a safety. Tulane held Flynn to 8-of-18 passing and limited LSU to a listless 11 yards on 12 carries. Meanwhile, the Wave put up 126 yards on the nation's No. 1 defense and drove 58 yards in 11 plays for a touchdown and 9-7 lead with 1:40 to go before halftime.

"Nobody's a six-touchdown favorite," first-year

Tulane coach Bob Toledo said he told his players before the game.

"There's no way they're a 40-point favorite."

That was painfully obvious for LSU as Tulane's sideline rocked late in the second quarter as if it had won. LSU's heads were down and Miles was grimacing.

"Goliath was a 40-point favorite, too, but David hit him right between the eyes," Toledo said.

LSU was still stunned on its way to the lockers at the half even though it was ahead 10-9 after driving 37 yards for a 36-yard field goal by Colt David with three seconds left in the second quarter. The Tigers may have gotten a touchdown, but wide receiver Brandon LaFell dropped two passes right to him from Flynn. Then Flynn nearly threw an interception in the end zone.

LSU was winning, but its body language said it was losing. Tulane was losing, but it basically flew to the locker room. So much so that game officials had to slow the Greenies down as they rushed up the back of the Tigers as both teams exited via the same portal.

"Yeah, they were heckling us," LSU cornerback Chevis Jackson said. "They were telling us we were overrated. They were trying to get under our skin."

It was working. LSU drew a season-high 11 penalties for a game in the first half alone with most of those on the offense. Tulane tailback Matt Forte had 38 yards on 11 carries, and Gabe Ratcliff had dented that vaunted defense for three receptions for 31 yards.

"Halftime was good," Toledo said. "We had LSU going."

But finally, LSU woke up.

"We've seen their best game," Miles said. "Now, we have to play our best game."

Left: LSU quarterback Matt Flynn (15) tries to avoid the Tulane pass rush during the Tigers' 34-9 win over the Green Wave.
Photo by Alex Brandon/AP

Opposite: LSU running back Trindon Holliday (8) eludes the Tulane defense during the Tigers' win in the Superdome.
Photo by Alex Brandon/AP

That started with the running game. LSU put up 123 yards on 26 carries in the second half with tailback Charles Scott getting 53 on six carries, including a 35-yard touchdown run in the fourth quarter for a 27-9 lead and a 3-yard scoring run for the final.

Tailback Jacob Hester got it started with LSU's first possession of the second half as he ripped runs of 6 and 14 yards. Then backup quarterback Ryan Perrilloux entered for the first time and gained 10 yards around end. Flynn, who finished a strong 16-of-29 for 258 yards with one interception, found receiver Chris Mitchell for 15 yards. This led to a 33-yard field goal by David for a 13-9 lead.

Then Tulane deflated. On its second play of the second half, Forte fumbled after a hit by linebacker Luke Sanders and tackle Al Woods recovered at the Tulane 48. Flynn hit receiver Terrance Toliver for 38 yards to set up a 1-yard touchdown run by Hester and a 20-9 lead with 5:53 to play in the third quarter. Hester had put LSU up 7-0 in the first quarter on a 3-yard run before Tulane drew within 7-2 on the safety.

"Luke's hit and the fumble was the turning point," Jackson said. "They were excited before that. Then we played our brand of football. We weren't down. We just had to play better."

Leave it to a neighbor to tell LSU a cautionary tale.

"No matter who it is, you've got to go out and play," Scott said. "Tulane, Florida, it doesn't matter. We were kind of looking ahead."

Florida will be Saturday at 7:30 p.m. on CBS in Tiger Stadium.

"We'll be ready for next week," Miles said.

"This is definitely something that can't happen again," Hester said. "It can't happen next week or we'll lose." ∎

#2 LSU vs. Tulane

September 29, 2007 | New Orleans, LA

SCORING SUMMARY

Team	1st	2nd	3rd	4th	End
LSU	7	3	10	14	34
Tulane	0	9	0	0	9

First quarter
LSU – Jacob Hester 3 run (Colt David kick) 10:56

Second quarter
TUL – Safety 5:56
TUL – Andre Anderson 5 run (Ross Thevenot kick) 1:40
LSU – David 36 field goal   :03

Third quarter
LSU – David 33 field goal 8:51
LSU – Hester 1 run (David kick) 5:53

Fourth quarter
LSU – Charles Scott 35 run (David kick) 12:00
LSU – Scott 3 run (David kick) 8:49

TEAM STATS

	LSU	TU
First Downs	16	12
Rush-Pass-Penalty	7-9-0	6-6-0
Rushes-Yards	38-134	33-88
Passing Yards	257	139
Com-Att-Int	17-32-1	12-32-1
Total Plays	70	65
Total Yards	391	227
Avg. Gain Per Play	5.6	3.5
Fumbles: No.-Lost	1-0	2-2
Penalties: No.-Yards	15-91	4-23
Punts-Avg.	5-46.6	10-38.9
Punt Returns: No.-Yards	4-25	2-8
Kickoff Returns: No.-Yards	2-64	8-107
Interceptions: No.-Yards	1-0	1-0
Fumble Returns: No.-Yards	0-0	0-0
Possession Time	31:34	28:26
Third-Down Conv.	8-17	6-17
Fourth-Down Conv.	0-0	0-0
Sacks By: No.-Yards	2-13	6-44

INDIVIDUAL STATISTICS: LSU

Rushing	No	Yds	TD	Lg
Charles Scott	6	53	2	35
Richard Murphy	6	35	0	9
Jacob Hester	10	33	2	14
Trindon Holliday	3	19	0	12
Keiland Williams	4	19	0	14
Ryan Perrilloux	2	14	0	10
Matt Flynn	7	-39	0	5

Passing	Att	Com	Int	Yds	TD	Lg
Matt Flynn	29	16	1	258	0	43
Ryan Perrilloux	3	1	0	-1	0	0

Receiving	No	Yds	TD	Lg
Brandon LaFell	4	76	0	43
Demetrius Byrd	3	69	0	39
Chris Mitchell	3	32	0	16
Richard Dickson	2	25	0	19
Richard Murphy	2	0	0	1
Terrance Toliver	1	38	0	38
Jared Mitchell	1	17	0	17
Trindon Holliday	1	0	0	0

Punting	No.	Yds	Avg	Lg
Josh Jasper	1	40	40.0	40
Patrick Fisher	4	193	48.2	54

INDIVIDUAL STATISTICS: Tulane

Rushing	No	Yds	TD	Lg
Matt Forte	16	73	0	21
Andre Anderson	7	18	1	6
Anthony Scelfo	7	4	0	10
Shannon Davis	3	-7	0	1

Passing	Att	Com	Int	Yds	TD	Lg
Anthony Scelfo	26	11	1	117	0	24
Kevin Moore	5	1	0	22	0	22
Matt Forte	1	0	0	0	0	0

Receiving	No	Yds	TD	Lg
Gabe Ratcliff	4	55	0	24
Brian King	4	32	0	22
Matt Forte	1	21	0	21
Michael Batiste	1	20	0	20
Kenneth Guidroz	1	11	0	11
Jeremy McKinney	1	0	0	0

Punting	No	Yds	Avg	Lg
Ross Thevenot	10	389	38.9	55

LSU's Flynn plays through the pain

By Bob Heist | The Daily Advertiser

Matt Flynn acknowledged the obvious following his uneven performance in a 34-9 win against Tulane at the Louisiana Superdome.

LSU's starting quarterback isn't 100 percent back from a high right ankle sprain.

"No," the fifth-year senior said curtly when asked if he's operating without limitations.

Asked to expand on that answer and rate the level at which he's playing on a percentage basis, Flynn declined, just saying, "Close."

That, however, appears debatable since he suffered the injury three weeks ago during the second half of the Virginia Tech game. And the numbers suggested Flynn was limited far more than anyone let on with the program.

For instance: After sitting out the Middle Tennessee game, Flynn returned for last week's 28-16 win over South Carolina at Tiger Stadium and completed just 8 of 19 passes for a career-low 70 yards with one touchdown and one interception.

Left: A pair of LSU defenders wrap up a Tulane ballcarrier during the Tigers' 34-9 win over the Green Wave in the Superdome.
Photo by Alex Brandon/AP

47

Right: LSU wide receiver Demetrius Byrd (2) leaps over Tulane defender Josh Lumar in attempting to make a catch during the Tigers' win over the Green Wave.

Photo by Alex Brandon/AP

Opposite left: LSU wide receiver Brandon LaFell (1) tries to break away from Tulane safety Joe Goosby during the Tigers' 34-9 victory over the Green Wave.

Photo by Alex Brandon/AP

Opposite right: LSU's Jacob Hester (18) runs into the end zone for a Tigers' touchdown against Tulane.

Photo by Alex Brandon/AP

Those struggles were magnified in the first half against Tulane. Until completing 4 of 7 passes for 53 yards and driving LSU to the go-ahead field goal just before halftime, Flynn hit on only four of his first 11 passes and was sacked four times.

At that point — including the second half against South Carolina — Flynn was mired in four mediocre quarters of football, having completed just 6 of 16 passes for 99 yards with no touchdowns and two interceptions. He had rushed nine times for minus-22 yards.

"We all talked at halftime, and as an offense, we told Matt we're behind him," said LSU's sophomore receiver Brandon LaFell. "It's just, Matt's not hurt — he's just a little timid on the ankle.

"The thing is, we know what Matt can do. There's no guesswork involved with him. It just takes time coming back from an injury like that."

To Flynn's credit, he rallied in the second half as LSU broke away, completing 8 of 11 passes for 120 yards. But his immobility remained an issue after being sacked two more times.

And what a bad combination the day was. LSU's offensive line played its worst game against a defense that's rated No. 94 nationally in total defense with an immobile quarterback. The six sacks of Flynn — who passed for 258 yards against Tulane —were the most by the Green Wave since recording six against SMU in 2005. LSU hadn't surrendered that many since Florida racked

up eight in 2001.

"There were a couple of times I would have liked to have gotten out a little faster, and that would have helped everything," said Flynn. "But the ankle's making progress and I'll be able to do those things soon."

But is "soon" soon enough with No. 4 Florida coming to Tiger Stadium this week?

"Matt's going to be fine," senior tailback Jacob Hester said. "What's important is he was there when he needed to be there today, and made big throws when he needed to make a big throw.

"Has it been perfect? Probably not. But he's our guy and he's going to be fine." ■

Florida

GAME SIX 10.6.07 ■ FLORIDA **24** | LSU **28**

Above: LSU head coach Les Miles makes his way into Tiger Stadium before the game against Florida.
Photo by Shane Bevel/The Times

Left: LSU linebacker Ali Highsmith, running backs coach Larry Porter, head coach Les Miles, and LSU defensive tackle Glenn Dorsey celebrate their 28-24 victory over the Florida Gators.
Photo by Shane Bevel/The Times

Dramatic fourth-quarter rally saves top-ranked LSU from upset

By Glenn Guilbeau | Louisiana Gannett News

LSU has the best tailgating in the country.

LSU has the loudest stadium in the country.

LSU has the best football in the country.

That last one is not up for argument at the moment.

The Tigers, ranked No. 1 in the country in season for the first time since 1959, looked every bit the part in front of 92,910 — the largest crowd in Tiger Stadium history — as they came from 10 points behind in the fourth quarter for a thrilling, one-for-the ages, 28-24 victory over No. 9 Florida.

With Harris poll and USA Today No. 1 USC (4-1) falling 24-23 to 40-point underdog Stanford, LSU (6-0) moved into No. 1 for the first time since 1959.

There were also another 57,000 fans outside the stadium, according to LSU Police estimates, and more cars in a three-mile radius of the stadium than ever before for a game.

In a game billed as perhaps the biggest in LSU history, virtually all got what they came for. Add it all up, and it may have been the greatest night in Tiger Stadium history.

"It's close if it's not the greatest," said LSU tailback Jacob Hester, who scored the winning touchdown on a 2-yard run on third-and-goal with 1:09 to play in the game. "I've never seen the fans quite like they were tonight I mean from the get-go. And they never stopped."

Hester, a senior from Shreveport, converted a fourth-and-1 from the LSU 49 and another one from the Florida 7 on the final drive that covered 60 yards in 15 plays and took up 8:11. LSU was 5-for-5 on fourth down conversions overall on this wild night.

"No offensive player wants to see the kicker come on the field," said Hester, who finished with a game-high 106 yards on 23 carries. "We're No. 1 now and it's really without any argument."

But it wasn't over after Hester's last touchdown.

Florida quarterback Tim Tebow, who passed for 158 yards and ran and scrambled for 67, rambled for a 21-yard gain to the LSU 45 with 12 seconds remaining. With five seconds remaining, he threw one last heave into the end zone, but it was batted away by defensive back Chad Jones to end the game.

LSU coach Les Miles called it a victory like no other.

"None," he said. "That team is a pretty special group of men. The character of this team was really displayed in front of that stadium. Pretty special game."

The Tigers cut it to 24-21 with 10:15 to play in the game on a daring fourth-and-3 play from the Florida 4. Quarterback Matt Flynn stepped to his right out of the pocket and found wide open receiver Demetrius Byrd for the 4-yard touchdown.

LSU defensive end Kirston Pittman's interception of a tipped pass from Tebow set up the Tigers at the Florida 27-yard line. He rebounded the ball off Florida tight end Cornelius Ingram.

LSU tailback Trindon Holliday gained 16 on a reverse, and after an incompletion, tailback Keiland Williams gained 9. On third-and-1, Williams lost 2 yards, bringing up the fourth-and-3.

Florida took a 24-14 lead with 5:16 to play in the third quarter on a 37-yard touchdown pass from Tebow to Ingram, who had no one near him for 20 yards in the LSU secondary as he benefited from an obvious blown coverage. The touchdown silenced the largest crowd in LSU history after it was roaring louder than perhaps ever before.

The Tigers, trailing 17-7 at the half, grabbed the momentum with the opening kickoff of the third quarter as they drove from their 30 to the Florida 25. On fourth-and-5, LSU faked a field goal as holder Flynn faked a placement and rambled 8 yards around end for a first down at the Gators' 17. Following a pass interference call against Florida that gave LSU a first-and-goal at the 3, Williams scored two plays later on a 4-yard run to cut Florida's lead to 17-14 with 7:49 to play in the third quarter.

Moments after the touchdown as the crowd was still celebrating the touchdown, Tiger Stadium public address

Above: LSU quarterback Perrilloux is congratulated by Matt Flynn after scoring LSU's only touchdown of the first half during the game at Tiger Stadium.
Photo by Shane Bevel/The Times

Left: LSU quarterback Ryan Perrilloux dances past Florida linebacker Ryan Stamper in the first half of the game to score LSU's only touchdown of the first half.
Photo by Shane Bevel/The Times

announcer Dan Borne announced that USC had just lost to unranked Stanford. The place went wild with deafening noise, and press box computers vibrated right along. Players on the LSU sideline began celebrating as if they had just won a game. Then Tebow directed the Gators to a 75-yard touchdown drive on five plays for the 10-point advantage.

LSU outgained Florida 177 yards to 172 in the first half but found itself down 17-7 at halftime after Colt David missed a 43-yard field goal wide right with 28 seconds to go in the second quarter. The miss wasted a 42-yard drive in nine plays.

LSU's offense sputtered throughout the first half as wide receiver Brandon LaFell continued to drop passes and Flynn misfired here and there.

The Tigers had drawn within 10-7 on a 1-yard touchdown run by backup quarterback Ryan Perrilloux on fourth-and-goal with 6:08 to play in the second period. The touchdown finished off an 80-yard drive in 16 plays in which Flynn completed 4 of 4 passes for 45 yards.

But LSU's vaunted defense could not stop or contain Tebow.

The dual-action sophomore completed 7 of 13 passes in the first half for 89 yards with a 2-yard touchdown pass and rushed and scrambled 13 times for 44 yards with a 9-yard touchdown run with 2:23 to go before half for the 17-7 advantage.

Tebow broke tackles, faked out defenders and threw on the run to frustrate the LSU defense, which appeared confused on the Gators' final drive of the half that covered 72 yards in 10 plays. The Gators took a 3-0 lead on their first possession of the game on a 31-yard field goal by Joey Ijjas. ∎

Above: LSU's Marlon Favorite (99) tackles Florida quarterback Tim Tebow. *Photo by Shane Bevel/The Times*

Left: LSU head coach Les Miles talks to an official after a touchdown run by Florida quarterback Tim Tebow in the first half. *Photo by Shane Bevel/The Times*

Far left: LSU quarterback Matt Flynn fires a pass away in the first half. *Photo by Shane Bevel/The Times*

Opposite: LSU wide receiver Brandon LaFell gets tripped up by Florida cornerback Wondy Pierre-Louis during the first half. *Photo by Shane Bevel/The Times*

#9 Florida v. #1 LSU

October 6, 2007 | Baton Rouge, LA

SCORING SUMMARY

Team	1st	2nd	3rd	4th	End
Florida	3	14	7	0	24
LSU	0	7	7	14	28

First quarter
UF – Joey Ijjas 31 field goal 11:19

Second quarter
UF – Kestahn Moore 2 pass from Tim Tebow (Ijjas kick) 13:45
LSU – Ryan Perrilloux 1 run (Colt David kick) 6:08
UF – Tebow 9 run (Ijjas kick) 2:23

Third quarter
LSU – Keiland Williams 4 run (David kick) 7:49
UF – Cornelius Ingram 37 pass from Tebow (Ijjas kick) 5:16

Fourth quarter
LSU – Demetrius Byrd 4 pass from Matt Flynn (David kick) 10:15
LSU – Jacob Hester 2 run (David kick) 1:09

TEAM STATS

TEAM STATS	UF	LSU
First Downs	19	25
Rush-Pass-Penalty	9-7-3	13-11-1
Rushes-Yards	32-156	52-247
Passing Yards	158	144
Com-Att-Int	12-26-1	14-28-1
Total Plays	58	80
Total Yards	314	391
Avg. Gain Per Play	5.4	4.9
Fumbles: No.-Lost	2-1	0-0
Penalties: No.-Lost	2-8	7-61
Punts-Avg	2-37.0	2-49.0
Punt Returns: No.-Yards	1-17	0-0
Kickoff Returns: No.-Yards	3-24	4-89
Interceptions: No.-Yards	1-10	1-0
Fumble Returns: No.-Yards	0-0	0-0
Possession Time	24:08	35:52
Third-Down Conv.	6-9	8-17
Fourth-Down Conv.	0-0	5-5
Sacks By: No.-Yards	0-0	2-8

INDIVIDUAL STATS: Florida

Rushing	No.	Yds	TD	Lg
Kestahn Moore	12	79	0	17
Tim Tebow	16	67	1	21
Percy Harvin	3	11	0	6

INDIVIDUAL STATS: Florida

Passing	Att	Cmp	Int	Yds	TD	Lg
Tim Tebow	26	12	1	158	2	37

Receiving	No.	Yds	TD	Lg
Percy Harvin	4	58	0	27
Louis Murphy	3	26	0	12
Cornelius Ingram	2	43	1	37
Kestahan Moore	2	21	1	19
Andre Caldwell	1	10	0	10

Punting	No.	Yds	Avg	Lg
Chas Henry	2	74	37.0	40

INDIVIDUAL STATS: LSU

Rushing	No.	Yds	TD	Lg
Jacob Hester	23	106	1	19
Keiland Williams	9	46	1	21
Trindon Holliday	6	33	0	16
Matt Flynn	4	30	0	15
Ryan Perrilloux	6	23	1	9
Charles Scott	4	9	0	4

Passing	Att	Cmp	Int	Yds	TD
Matt Flynn	27	14	1	144	1
Ryan Perrilloux	1	0	0	0	0

Receiving	No.	Yds	TD	Lg
Brandon LaFell	6	73	0	16
Demetrius Byrd	3	20	1	12
Jared Mitchell	2	30	0	18
Richard Dickson	1	14	0	14
Charles Scott	1	6	0	6
Keiland Williams	1	1	0	1

Punting	No.	Yds	Avg	Lg
Patrick Fisher	2	98	49.0	55

Right: Kestahn Moore celebrates a Florida touchdown after beating the LSU defense on a short pass play in the first half of the game at Tiger Stadium.

Photo by Shane Bevel/The Times

Above: LSU's Trindon Holliday runs past the Florida defense.
Photo by Shane Bevel/The Times

Right: Rabid LSU fans turned out by the tens of thousands for the game against Florida at Tiger Stadium. *Photo by Shane Bevel/The Times*

Far right: LSU's defense pursues Florida quarterback Tim Tebow. *Photo by Shane Bevel/The Times*

Opposite: LSU Chevis Jackson, Joshua McManus and Chad Jones work to breakup the final Hail Mary of the game against Florida and secure the victory for the Tigers.
Photo by Shane Bevel/The Times

High-priced event pays dividends with classic

By Bob Tompkins | The Town Talk

Well, they sure got their money's worth.

Tickets were scalped for more than $1,000 for the brawl between No. 1 LSU and No. 9 Florida, and it was a college football classic that lived up to its incredible pregame hype before a record crowd of 92,910 thunderous fans.

And the outcome, for LSU, was priceless.

LSU, converting five straight gutsy fourth downs — four in the second half — rallied three times from 10-point deficits, at 10-0, 17-7 and 24-14, to pull out a 28-24 victory that went down to the wire.

When Chad Jones broke up Tim Tebow's 46-yard bomb into the end zone on the final play, LSU's No. 1 Tigers became the only No. 1 team in the land.

And they did so against a team led by a brash, bruising sophomore quarterback that looks like the best college football player in the country.

Not since Archie Manning almost single-handedly beat LSU in 1968 and '69 has a quarterback given LSU as many fits as Tebow, with both his scrambling, bullish runs and his left-handed passing.

Earlier, it appeared LSU started celebrating too early— after word that the Trojans of USC, the only other top-ranked team in the land, had fallen.

LSU had just scored to cap a nice opening drive of the second half to pull within 17-14 of ninth-ranked Florida when word came over the public address system that Stanford had beaten USC, the No. 1 team in the USA Today Coaches poll. USC, of course, is LSU's hated nemesis since splitting the national championship with the Tigers in 2003, by a 24-23 score.

It was as if a jet buzzed the stadium for all the noise that erupted while the Tigers were jumping up and down and waving from the sidelines.

The defending national champion upset last week by Auburn, and its bruising sophomore quarterback, promptly drove down LSU's gut for a 24-14 lead.

Great teams don't wither in such circumstances, and the Tigers showed why they are worthy, for now anyway, of being No. 1 with their valiant comeback.

One commentator on a Baton Rouge radio station before the game said this was the biggest game in LSU football history. If he said it once, he must have said it a hundred times.

All right, already. We got the point. No need to run this into the ground.

Yes, it was a big, big game, as everybody already knew, but these kind of proclamations are best made after the fact. With a clear head and with hindsight, people can better make such a statement after the appropriate comparisons. (No. 1 LSU vs. No. 3 Ole Miss on Halloween Night in 1959 was no slouch.)

If there was any way to whip fans of the top-ranked Tigers into a bigger frenzy before the game, I don't know what it could've been, short of a Super Bowl-type pregame show.

This was the night when Mike VI, the Tigers' new mascot, made his debut in Tiger Stadium as the cheerleaders wheeled him around the field in his cage to great cheering, especially from the students.

There were 10 top-10 matchups in this storied stadium before this year, and now this was the second of the season (No. 2 LSU whipped No. 9 Virginia Tech 48-7 last month) and the 12th overall.

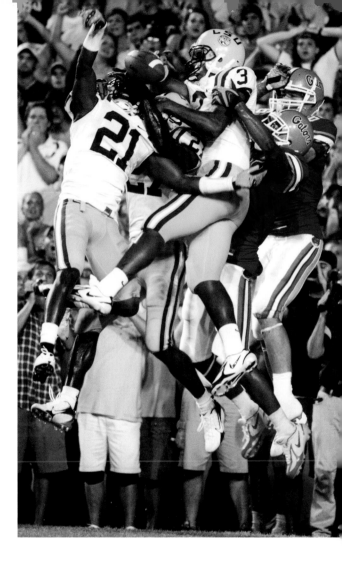

It was "Looziana Saturday Night," with alligator sauce piquant being served in the press box, and a pregame salute to a Charles Barney, who pledged $4.7 million to the LSU Geology Department, and four guest captains, past LSU stars Charles Alexander, Max Fugler, Jerry Stovall and Maurice LeBlanc.

There were more fans and more cars on the LSU campus than ever in the history of the school. Judging from the pregame traffic, there must have been a ton who didn't get in but watched elsewhere. ∎

Kentucky

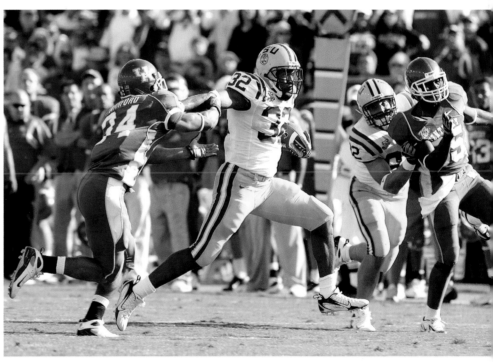

Above: LSU running back Charles Scott (32) pushes away from Kentucky's Paul Warford for a first-quarter gain against the Wildcats. *Photo by Randy Snyder/Special to The Times*

Left: LSU running back Jacob Hester is stopped by a host of Kentucky defenders during the second half of the Tigers' 43-37 triple-overtime loss. *Photo by Randy Snyder/Special to The Times*

61

LSU sings the blues in loss to Kentucky

By Glenn Guilbeau | Louisiana Gannett News

Mighty No. 1 LSU ran out of miracles and fourth downs as Kentucky left the Tigers blue in the grass.

Five years after the most infamous loss in Kentucky football history dubbed the "Bluegrass Miracle," the No. 17 Wildcats returned the favor to LSU with their greatest home win ever, and this time it stuck.

No. 17 Kentucky stopped a fourth-and-2 play by the Tigers in triple overtime for its first home win against the No. 1 team in the nation — 43-37 over the Tigers in front of 70,902 at Commonwealth Stadium in four-and-a-half-hour marathon.

"I thought I was real close to getting it," said LSU tailback Charles Scott, who got the call on fourth-and-2 from the Kentucky 17 in the third overtime after the Wildcats had just taken a 43-37 lead on quarterback André Woodson's third touchdown pass.

"It was just a power play just to get the two yards," Scott said.

"Somehow the linebacker came free, and it was me and him, and he stopped me for one yard. He came out of nowhere."

Outside linebacker Braxton Kelley nailed Scott and LSU a yard short, ending its miraculous 6-for-6 fourth-down conversions streak and undefeated run as No. 1. Suddenly it was Midnight Madness in the early evening as Big Blue fans enveloped the field in seconds just 18 hours or so after the basketball team celebrated Midnight Madness practice.

"Having beat LSU, I go home with a high head for the rest of my life," Kentucky receiver and New Orleans native Dicky Lyons Jr. said. "It doesn't get much better than that."

Scott didn't believe what had happened at first. In one swoosh of blue, LSU's No. 1 ranking and the nation's longest winning streak of 13 games were done just one week after one of the Tigers' greatest home Saturday nights in history just last week in a 28-24 win over No. 9 Florida.

"It took a few seconds for it to hit me," Scott said. "I thought they were going to at least measure. But then when they stormed the field, I was like, 'Oh, man.' I know what it looked like. It just hurt."

Scott, who led all rushers with 94 yards on seven carries, had given LSU a seemingly comfortable 17-7 lead on a 13-yard touchdown run with 1:48 to play in the second quarter. But Woodson completed a 51-yard pass to Steve Johnson and scrambled for a 12-yard touchdown to cut the Tigers' lead to 17-14 with 1:04 to go before halftime.

LSU (6-1, 3-1 Southeastern Conference) took another seemingly comfortable, 27-14 lead late in the third quarter on a 30-yard field goal by Colt David.

"I just can't say enough about these young men," Kentucky coach Rich Brooks said. "Whenever it starts to look dark, that's when they dig down and find something extra. They did it again tonight."

Kentucky (6-1, 2-1 SEC) had little problem with the No. 1 defense in the land and scored 13 unanswered points on a touchdown and two field goals. Lones Seiber tied it 27-27 with 4:21 to play on a 27-yard field goal.

"I can tell you I'm surprised how well Kentucky moved the football," LSU coach Les Miles said after watching his defense surrender a season-high 375 yards with 333 by the end of regulation.

LSU's No. 1 ranking in defense could likely also fall along with its No. 1 ranking in pass efficiency defense. Woodson completed 21 of 38 passes for 250 yards and three touchdowns with two interceptions. LSU quarterback Matt Flynn was no match as he completed 17 of 35 passes for 130 yards with one interception and several misfires.

"We've got a team that's sick," Miles said of the loss. "Did not enjoy this."

LSU drove toward the winning points as the fourth quarter elapsed, but Flynn continued to miss receivers and the drive stalled at the Kentucky 40. David tried a 57-yard field goal with two seconds left and had the length, but it sailed wide left to bring on overtime.

"It felt pretty solid," David said. "Then I looked up and saw it trailing. I hit one from about 57 in practice this week."

Kentucky got the ball first at the LSU 25 and scored in five plays on a 1-yard run by tailback Derrick Locke, who gained 64 yards on 20 carries for the game. The Tigers scored in four plays on a 2-yard run by tailback Richard Murphy to tie it 34-34. LSU kept possession but was held to a 38-yard field goal by David for a 37-34 advantage. Then Kentucky was held to a 43-yard field goal by Seiber for a 37-37 deadlock.

Kentucky retained possession and LSU apparently forced another field goal when a third-and-goal pass by Woodson fell incomplete, but LSU safety Curtis Taylor was guilty of holding. Kentucky got a first-and-goal at the 3, and after a delay of game penalty, Woodson found Johnson for a 7-yard touchdown pass. The mandatory 2-point conversion by the third overtime failed as Kentucky led 43-37.

LSU tailback Jacob Hester, who had 62 yards on 18 carries, gained six on first down before getting zero and then 2 yards, bringing up the fourth-and-2 play and Scott.

"Felt like we had an advantage there," Miles said. "We should've got two."

But No. 1 just got one. There would be no miracle pass this time as in LSU's 33-30 win here in 2002. ∎

Above: LSU's Chevis Jackson (21) was mobbed by teammates after intercepting an Andre Woodson pass during the Tigers' triple-overtime loss at Kentucky. *Photo by Sam Upshaw Jr./The Courier-Journal*

Opposite top: Kentucky coach Rich Brooks has some words for the officials during LSU's 43-37 triple-overtime loss to the Wildcats. *Photo by Pat McDonogh/The Courier-Journal*

Opposite middle: LSU's cheerleaders cheer their team against Kentucky. *Photo by Randy Snyder/Special to The Times*

Opposite bottom: LSU head coach Les Miles looks on during the Tigers' loss at Kentucky. *Photo by Sam Upshaw Jr./The Courier-Journal*

#1 LSU vs. #17 Kentucky

October 13, 2007 | Lexington, KY

SCORING SUMMARY

Team	1st	2nd	3rd	4th	OT	End
LSU	0	17	10	0	10	37
Kentucky	7	7	7	6	16	43

First Quarter
UK – T.C. Drake 2 pass from Andre Woodson (Lones Seiber kick) 2:49

Second Quarter
LSU – Charles Scott 1 run (Colt David kick) 14:55
LSU – David 31 field goal 5:42
LSU – Scott 13 run (David kick) 1:48
UK – Woodson 12 run (Seiber kick) 1:04

Third Quarter
LSU – Richard Dickson 4 pass from Matt Flynn (David kick) 9:12
LSU – David 30 field goal 3:49
UK – Jacob Tamme 8 pass from Woodson (Seiber kick) 1:13

Fourth Quarter
UK – Seiber 33 field goal (7:57)
UK – Seiber 27 field goal (4:210)

Overtime
UK – Derrick Locke 1 run (Seiber kick) 15:00
LSU – Richard Murphy 2 run (David kick) 15:00
LSU – David 38 field goal 15:00
UK – Seiber 43 field goal 15:00
UK – Steve Johnson 7 pass from Woodson (kick failed) 15:00

TEAM STATS

	LSU	UK
First Downs	22	24
Rush-Pass-Penalty	12-7-3	8-13-3
Rushes-Yards	50-261	41-125
Passing Yards	142	250
Com-Att-Int	18-37-1	21-38-2
Total Plays	87	79
Total Yards	403	375
Avg. Gain Per Play	4.6	4.7
Fumbles: No.-Lost	0-0	3-0
Penalties: No.-Yards	12-103	7-62
Punts-Avg.	4-33.8	3-47.3
Punt Returns: No.-Yards	0-0	1-1
Kickoff Returns: No.-Yards	6-401	6-389
Interceptions: No.-Yards	2-0	1-0
Possession Time	33:21	26:39
Third-Down Conv.	8-19	9-17
Fourth-Down Conv.	1-2	1-1
Sacks By: No.-Yards	0-0	3-15

INDIVIDUAL STATS: LSU

Rushing

	No	Yds	TD	Lg
Charles Scott	7	94	2	55
Jacob Hester	18	61	0	11
Matt Flynn	10	53	0	22
Trindon Holliday	5	24	0	17
Ryan Perrilloux	5	15	0	10
Richard Murphy	3	10	1	5
Keiland Williams	1	5	0	5
Terrance Toliver	1	-1	0	0

Passing

	Att	Com	Int	Yds	TD	Lg
Matt Flynn	35	17	1	130	1	18
Ryan Perrilloux	2	1	0	12	0	12

Receiving

	No.	Yds	TD	Lg
Brandon LaFell	4	42	0	18
Richard Dickson	4	33	1	12
Richard Murphy	2	22	0	14
Jared Mitchell	2	9	0	9
Charles Scott	2	6	0	5
Demetrius Byrd	1	13	0	13
Chris Mitchell	1	8	0	8
Keiland Williams	1	5	0	5
Jacob Hester	1	4	0	4

Punting

	No.	Yds	Avg	Lg
Patrick Fisher	4	135	33.8	43

INDIVIDUAL STATS: Kentucky

Rushing

	No	Yds	TD	Lg
Derrick Locke	20	64	1	17
Tony Dixon	17	45	0	11
Andre Woodson	3	16	1	12

Passing

	Att	Com	Int	Yds	TD	Lg
Andre Woodson	38	21	2	250	3	51

Receiving

	No.	Yds	TD	Lg
Steve Johnson	7	134	1	51
Dicky Lyons	6	49	0	14
Jacob Tamme	3	33	1	14
Keenan Burton	2	13	0	9
Tony Dixon	1	18	0	18
T.C. Drake	1	2	1	2
Maurice Grinter	1	1	0	1

Punting

	No.	Yds	Avg	Lg
Tim Masthay	3	142	47.3	59

Above: LSU's Craig Steltz, right, stops Kentucky's Tony Dixon during the first half at Commonwealth Stadium in Lexington, Ky.
Photo by Randy Snyder/Special to The Times

Left top: Kentucky quarterback Andre Woodson prepares to throw with LSU's Tyson Jackson (93) bearing down on him.
Photo by Pat McDonogh/The Courier-Journal

Left bottom: Kentucky's Sam Maxwell, left, rushes in as LSU quarterback Matt Flynn pitches the ball to Jacob Hester during the second half at Commonwealth Stadium in Lexington, Ky.
Photo by Randy Snyder/Special to The Times

Opposite top: Kentucky's Trevard Lindley (right) breaks up a pass intended for LSU's Terrance Toliver during the Tigers' 43-37 triple-overtime loss. *Photo by Sam Upshaw Jr./The Courier-Journal*

Opposite bottom: Kentucky quarterback Andre Woodson scores on a 12-yard touchdown run in the second quarter of the Wildcats' win over No. 1 LSU. *Photo by Sam Upshaw Jr./The Courier-Journal*

Passing game mistakes cost Tigers

By John Marcase | The Town Talk

Top-ranked LSU opened the second half of its 43-37 overtime loss to No. 17 Kentucky on the verge of delivering a knockout blow.

Tight end Richard Dickson had just caught a 4-yard touchdown pass from Matt Flynn to allow the Tigers to extend their 17-14 halftime lead to 24-14.

On Kentucky's ensuing possession, LSU backup safety Chad Jones made a diving interception of Andre Woodson. It was the Tigers' second pick of Woodson, who earlier this season set the NCAA record for most pass attempts without a pick

The Tigers took over on their 49 and began driving into the end of the field where the large LSU crowd on hand in Commonwealth Stadium was located. LSU quickly moved into the red zone, but faced a third-and-8 from the 13.

Flynn rolled to his left and drew two defenders, allowing tight end Keith Zinger to roam free in the back of end zone. Flynn fired, but the ball just grazed off the fingertips of a leaping Zinger. Instead of a possible 17-point lead, LSU settled for a 30-yard field by Colt David, the second of three he would make.

The Tigers would not score again in regulation as Kentucky reeled off 20 consecutive points, including the first score in overtime.

The incompletion to Zinger was one of several

Above: LSU's Charles Scott (32) rambles for a big gain to set up the Tigers' first touchdown against Kentucky.
Photo by Pat McDonogh/The Courier-Journal

Left: LSU's Ali Highsmith, left, and Tyson Jackson, right, stop Kentucky's Tony Dixon during the first half at Commonwealth Stadium in Lexington, Ky. *Photo by Randy Snyder/Special to The Times*

Far left: LSU quarterback Matt Flynn drops back for a pass against Kentucky during the first half at Commonwealth Stadium in Lexington, Ky. *Photo by Randy Snyder/Special to The Times*

missed opportunities for an LSU offense that dominated the first three quarters. The Tigers held the ball for 10:10 of the second quarter and 11:11 of the third, but missed their chance at putting the Cats away, mainly due to miscues in the passing game.

Kentucky's field goal that tied the game at 27-27 with 2:47 left in regulation was set up by a Flynn interception when he underthrew an open Brandon LaFell.

"I didn't hold it too long," said Flynn. "It was just a bad throw."

Flynn, who was sacked three times, finished 17-of-35 for 130 yards, including 5-of-14 for 28 yards in the first half.

"We had a couple of things we thought were open," said LSU coach Les Miles. "We tried three to four deep throws where we thought we had an advantage and didn't make it."

LSU was also hurt by dropped passes as the Tigers essentially played their fifth straight game without leading receiver Early Doucet, who is still recovering from a groin injury. Doucet didn't play Saturday until LSU's final possession.

Another key miscue in the passing game nullified a first down inside the 10 in overtime as freshman Terrance Toliver was called for illegal touching when he lined up wrong. LSU eventually settled for a field goal.

"When you drop the football, you don't move the chains and it puts pressure on your defense," said Miles. "When we did make plays, we got penalized."

"They just made some plays," said Flynn. "We had a good week of practice. There was any letdown" following LSU's 28-24 win over Florida last week. "We just didn't execute." ∎

Right: LSU's Terrance Toliver, left, beats Kentucky's Paul Warford for a pass reception during the first half at Commonwealth Stadium in Lexington, Ky. LSU was penalized on the play.
Photo by Randy Snyder/Special to The Times

Far right: LSU quarterback Matt Flynn races away from Kentucky's Dominic Lewis during the first half on Saturday, Oct. 13, 2007, at Commonwealth Stadium in Lexington, Ky.
Photo by Randy Snyder/Special to The Times

Above: Kentucky wide receiver Steve Johnson catches what proves to be the game-winning touchdown against LSU. *Photo by Pat McDonogh/The Courier-Journal*

Left: LSU kicker Colt David reacts after missing a 57-yard field goal attempt that would have won the game for the Tigers. *Photo by Randy Snyder/Special to The Times*

Opposite top: LSU's Charles Scott is stopped on the last play of the game, ensuring a Kentucky victory in three overtimes. *Photo by Pat McDonogh/The Courier-Journal*

Opposite bottom: Kentucky coach Rich Brooks holds up his hands in victory after his team's win over LSU. *Photo by Pat McDonogh/The Courier-Journal*

Opposite right: LSU running back Charles Scott squats down after the Tigers lost 43-37 to Kentucky in three overtimes. *Photo by Randy Snyder/Special to The Times*

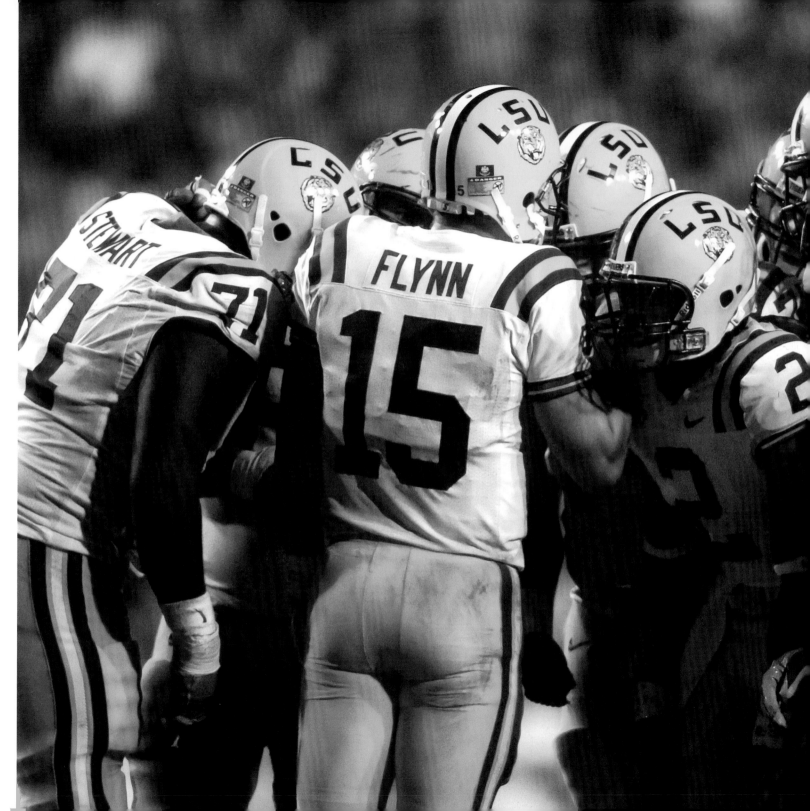

Auburn

GAME EIGHT 10.20.07 ■ AUBURN **24** | LSU **30**

Above: LSU players celebrate with Keiland Williams (5). *Photo by Jim Hudelson/The Times*

Left: Matt Flynn calls the play in the LSU huddle. *Photo by Jim Hudelson/The Times*

LSU survives scare from Auburn

By Glenn Guilbeau | Louisiana Gannett News

LSU finally found a receiver who can catch, and just in the nick of time.

Quarterback Matt Flynn, plagued by dropped passes all season, threw a 22-yard touchdown pass to Demetrius Byrd in the corner of the end zone with 1 second left for a 30-24 victory over No. 18 Auburn in front of 92,630 on another wild night in Tiger Stadium.

Byrd was well covered by cornerback Jerraud Powers, but he wrestled the ball away and held on for the game winner. Had it taken a second longer and had he not held on, Auburn would have won 24-23. It appeared No. 5 LSU (7-1) was playing for a game-winning field goal, but it let more than 20 seconds run off the clock before Flynn finally got the snap with a second to spare on the play clock.

The victory kept the Tigers in the national championship hunt as the No. 4 BCS team and put coach Les Miles' Tigers in a tie with Alabama for the Southeastern Conference West lead at 4-1. The Tigers play at Alabama (6-2, 4-1 SEC) and against former LSU coach Nick Saban on Nov. 3. Fans were chanting, "We want Saban," following the game.

Auburn (5-3, 3-2 SEC) scored its first points of the second half to take a 24-23 lead with 3:21 left in the fourth quarter on a 3-yard touchdown pass from quarterback Brandon Cox to wide receiver Rod Smith with the extra point by Wes Byrum.

Auburn had allowed 16 straight points by LSU in the

second half in falling behind 23-17. Cox took Auburn 83 yards in nine plays for the go-ahead score. The drive was aided by a 15-yard personal foul call against LSU safety Craig Steltz that gave Auburn a first down at Auburn's 41-yard line. Cox also converted a third-and-4 with an 11-yard completion to tailback Brad Lester, who then added a 15-yard reception and run to the LSU 8-yard line.

The Tigers took their first lead of the game with 12:55 to play in the fourth quarter at 20-17 on a 5-yard touchdown pass on third-and-goal from Flynn to tailback Jacob Hester.

Hester caught the ball inside at the 3-yard line and fought his way in. Flags were thrown near the play and it looked like LSU may not have gotten the play off in time, but after a review officials waved off the flags and signaled touchdown to a thunderous roar from the crowd.

Flynn, who hit tight end Richard Dickson for a 25-yard gain to the Auburn 30, directed LSU on an 85-yard drive in eight plays for the go-ahead score.

The Tigers extended the lead to 23-17 on a 33-yard field goal by Colt David with 8:12 to play in the game, capping a 55-yard drive in seven plays. Wide receiver Early Doucet, playing an appreciable amount of time for the first time since the second week of the season because of a groin injury, caught passes of 17 and 9 yards on the drive.

LSU drew within 17-13 on a 26-yard field goal by David with 2:03 to play in the third quarter. Flynn threw perfectly to Byrd on a 58-yard bomb to set the Tigers up with a first and goal at the 9. After three shots into the end zone, LSU kicked the field goal.

Doucet picked a crucial time to make his first big catch. Trailing 17-7 and facing a third-and-9 from its 32-yard line on its first possession of the second half, Doucet made a diving catch in double coverage for a 34-yard gain to the Auburn 34. Terrance Toliver then

Left: LSU's Demetrius Byrd (2) and Terrance Toliver reach for the football. *Photo by Jim Hudelson/The Times*

gained 17 on a reverse. The drive stalled, but David booted a 29-yard field goal to get LSU within 17-10 with 11:07 to play in the third period.

LSU found itself down 17-7 at the first half thanks to a critical fumble by backup quarterback Ryan Perrilloux at the LSU 39-yard line that turned into an Auburn touchdown and a 22-yard field goal by Byrum that followed a 90-yard drive in 12 plays.

The Tigers had the momentum of a 7-7 ballgame and the ball after just forcing a punt and getting a 14-yard return from Chad Jones and a 10-yard run from tailback Charles Scott to the LSU 34-yard line. Perrilloux ran left on an option holding the ball with two hands at his chest. Strong safety Zac Etheridge hit Perrilloux and the ball popped up. Powers grabbed the ball out of the air and rambled 36 yards to the LSU 3-yard line. On third-and-goal, fullback Carl Stewart pushed in from a yard out for the touchdown and a 14-7 lead with 9:34 to go before halftime.

LSU got excellent field position at its 41 following a 29-yard kickoff and drove to the Auburn 39, but the drive stalled. Patrick Fisher placed a punt at the Auburn 5, but Cox moved his Tigers 90 yards in 12 plays for the 22-yard field goal by Byrum.

Tailback Keiland Williams tied the game at 7 when he took a short screen pass from Flynn and raced 46 yards for a touchdown, badly faking out safety Erick Brock near the 10-yard line and waltzing in with 3:19 to play in the first quarter. ■

Right: Terrance Toliver (80) reaches for the football.
Photo by Jim Hudelson/The Times

Opposite: LSU's Matt Flynn (15) is brought down by the Auburn defense. *Photo by Jim Hudelson/The Times*

#17 Auburn vs. #4 LSU

October 20, 2007 | Baton Rouge, LA

SCORING SUMMARY

Team	1st	2nd	3rd	4th	End
Auburn	7	10	0	7	24
LSU	7	0	6	17	30

First quarter
AU – Montez Billings 17 pass from Brandon Cox (Wes Byrum kick) 10:10
LSU – Keiland Williams 46 pass from Matt Flynn (Colt David kick) 3:19

Second quarter
AU – Carl Stewart 1 run (Byrum kick) 9:34
AU – Wes Byrum 22 field goal 1:40

Third quarter
LSU – Colt David 29 field goal 11:21
LSU – David 26 field goal 2:03

Fourth quarter
LSU – Jacob Hester 5 pass from Flynn (David kick) 12:55
LSU – David 33 field goal 8:12
AU – Rod Smith 3 pass from Cox (Byrum kick) 3:21
LSU – Demetrius Byrd 22 pass from Flynn (David kick) 0:01

TEAM STATS

TEAM STATS	AUB	LSU
First Downs	16	23
Rush-Pass-Penalty	6-9-1	11-11-1
Rushes-Yards	35-97	33-169
Passing Yards	199	319
Com-Att-Int	18-28-0	22-35-1
Total Plays	63	68
Total Yards	296	488
Avg. Gain Per Play	4.7	7.2
Fumbles: No.-Lost	0-0	3-1
Penalties: No.-Yards	3-20	5-35
Punts-Avg.	7-43.1	4-52.0
Punt Returns: No.-Yards	0-0	4-35
Kickoff Returns: No.-Yards	7-135	3-6
Interceptions: No.-Yards	0-0	2-19
Fumble Returns: No.-Yards	1-8	0-0
Possession Time	32:44	27:16
Third-Down Conv.	6-14	7-15
Fourth-Down Conv.	0-0	0-0
Sacks By: No. Yards	2-18	2-9

INDIVIDUAL STATISTICS: Auburn

Rushing	No.	Yds	TD	Lg
Brad Lester	16	68	0	13
Ben Tate	10	17	0	6
Brandon Cox	6	12	0	9
Carl Stewart	1	1	1	1
Kodi Burns	1	1	0	1

INDIVIDUAL STATISTICS: Auburn

Passing	Att	Com	Int	Yds	TD	Lg
Brandon Cox	28	18	0	199	2	31

Receiving	No.	Yds	TD	Lg
Montez Billings	6	78	1	31
Rod Smith	6	56	1	19
Brad Lester	5	56	0	18
Mario Fannin	1	9	0	9

Punting	No.	Yds	Avg	Lg
Ryan Shoemaker	5	210	42.0	53
Patrick Tatum	2	92	46.0	46

INDIVIDUAL STATISTICS: LSU

Rushing	No.	Yds	TD	Lg
Jacob Hester	9	50	0	20
Matt Flynn	10	34	0	18
Charles Scott	5	28	0	17
Trindon Holliday	1	17	0	17
Terrance Toliver	1	17	0	17
Ryan Perrilloux	4	11	0	5
Keiland Williams	1	6	0	6
Richard Murphy	2	6	0	3

Passing	Att	Cmp	Int	Yds	TD	Lg
Matt Flynn	34	22	1	319	3	58
Ryan Perrilloux	1	0	0	0	0	0

Receiving	No.	Yds	TD	Lg
Early Doucet	7	93	0	33
Demetrius Byrd	3	89	1	58
Richard Dickson	3	31	0	25
Brandon LaFell	3	18	0	13
Terrance Toliver	2	19	0	13
Jacob Hester	2	6	1	5
Keiland Williams	1	46	1	46
Richard Murphy	1	17	0	17

Punting	No.	Yds	Avg	Lg
Patrick Fisher	4	208	52.0	55

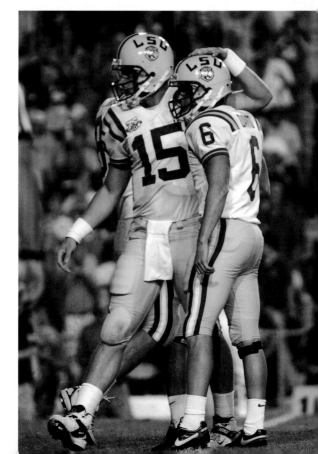

Above: LSU's Marlon Favorite (99) jumps into the air.
Photo by Jim Hudelson/The Times

Right: LSU's Matt Flynn (15) celebrates with Colt David after David's field goal.
Photo by Jim Hudelson/The Times

LSU win was magical—and weird, too

By Bob Tompkins | The Town Talk

Yes, magic can be found in this place called Death Valley. It was demonstrated again Saturday night. Did you see it? Could you believe it?

How many of the 92,630 fans here in Tiger Stadium and millions more in TV land, watching on ESPN, were frazzled and angry and bloated from munching on a bowlful of second-guesses when it happened?

How many Auburn fans were gloating and walking with a spring in their step when they capped an 83-yard, nine-play drive with a 3-yard touchdown pass from Brandon Cox to Rodgerious Smith with 3:21 remaining, and Wes Byrum's extra-point kick put 19th-ranked Auburn in front, 24-23.

And how many of them were shaking their heads in disbelief when it happened?

What happened came on third-and-8 from the Auburn 23. The ball was snapped with 10 seconds left. Matt Flynn passed the ball, and Demetrius Byrd caught it in the left corner of the end zone, beating sophomore

---

Top: LSU's Craig Steltz (16) and Danny McCray (44) make a tackle. *Photo by Jim Hudelson/The Times*

Far left: LSU's Jacob Hester (18) runs for yardage.
Photo by Jim Hudelson/The Times

Left: LSU quarterback Matt Flynn (15) is sacked by the Auburn defense. *Photo by Jim Hudelson/The Times*

cornerback Jerraud Powers.

And on the scoreboard, there was just 1 second left. Pandemonium.

Fifth-ranked LSU pulled a hat out of the bunny, beating Auburn 30-24. It was more than magical. It was weird.

Here was Auburn taking the opening drive of the contest down field for a touchdown, the first LSU foe to do that this season.

Later, with the score tied at 7, here was Ryan Perrilloux, LSU's backup quarterback who periodically goes into the game to run left, running left and having the ball jarred out of his hand and recovered in mid-air by Powers, who returned it 36 yards to the LSU 3, setting up a touchdown three plays later.

Later, there was LSU's defense, ranked second in the country in total defense and No. 1 in pass defense efficiency, allowing Auburn to march 90 yards in 12 plays for a field goal and a 10-point halftime lead.

And there was Brandon LaFell, running clear at about the Auburn 20, mimicking a 12-year-old trying to catch a long pass from his big brother. With a pass

that was sailing softly for his hands while he was open, he somehow knocked the ball up and into the hands of Auburn defender Patrick Lee.

On the next series, there was a pass Cox completed to a receiver at the sidelines that drew a flag and then a challenge. The flag was for holding and the challenge reversed the call, ruling no catch because it was out of bounds.

And, with LSU trailing 17-13, there was a flag thrown just before Flynn and Jacob Hester combined on a 5-yard touchdown that also drew a challenge. The refs announced there shouldn't have been a flag, based on the replay for the challenge review, and let the touchdown call stand.

The Tigers couldn't stand prosperity when, with a 23-17 lead, they again allowed Auburn to march down field, going 83 yards in nine plays for that go-ahead touchdown that seemed to be the clincher.

Yet, on the night Early Doucet returned with some great catches, it was Richard Murphy barely getting a first down and Flynn and Byrd pulling off a play that added a chapter to a rivalry replete with bizarre plays. ∎

Right: LSU's Jonathan Zenon (19) pulls down Auburn's Rodgeriqus Smith (80). *Photo by Jim Hudelson/The Times*

Far right: LSU's Early Doucet (9) celebrates late in the win over Auburn Saturday night at Tiger Stadium in Baton Rouge, Louisiana. *Photo by Jim Hudelson/The Times*

Opposite top: LSU's Matt Flynn and Early Doucet (9) celebrate. *Photo by Jim Hudelson/The Times*

Opposite bottom: LSU's Demetrius Byrd (2) and Tremaine Johnson celebrate the win over Auburn. *Photo by Jim Hudelson/The Times*

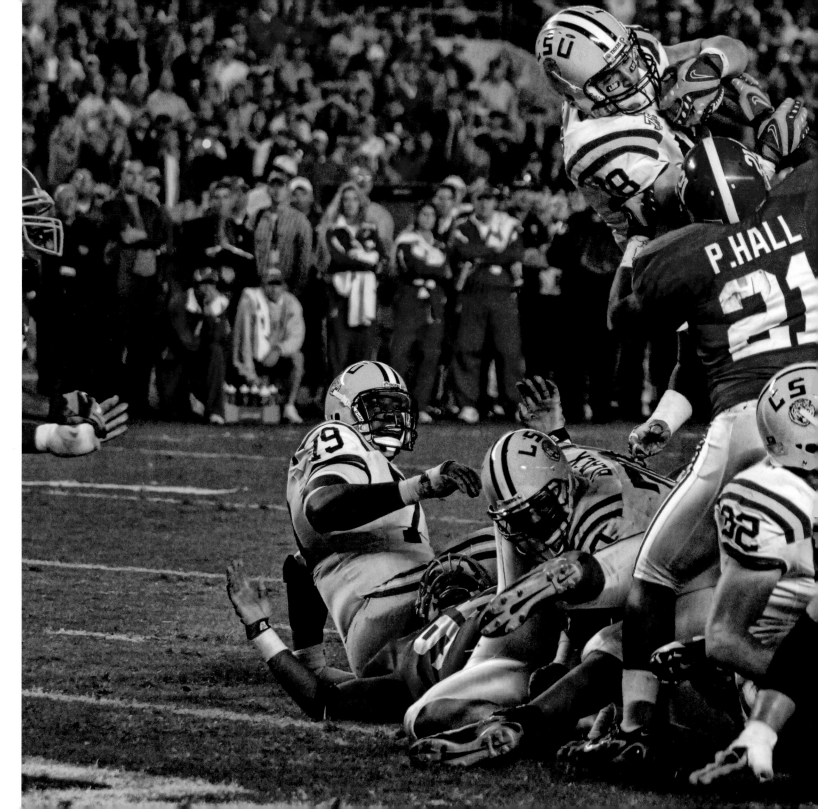

Alabama

Above: LSU wide receiver Early Doucet (9) hauls in a first-quarter touchdown pass against Alabama.
Photo by Tim Eddington/Special to The Times

Left: LSU running back Jacob Hester (18) dives over the pile for the game-winning touchdown against Alabama. *Photo by Tim Eddington/Special to The Times*

83

Tigers' rally lifts them past Saban, Alabama

By Glenn Guilbeau | Louisiana Gannett News

Everywhere you looked, there were Nick Saban signees making huge plays for his old LSU team and his new Alabama team, but in the end it was a Les Miles player that delivered LSU from evil.

Safety Chad Jones, a true freshman signee of the LSU coach, blitzed Alabama quarterback John Parker Wilson, sacked him and forced a fumble with 1:39 left that led to the winning touchdown and a 41-34 Tigers win in front of 92,138 at a hellish Bryant-Denny Stadium.

Fellow safety Curtis Taylor recovered Wilson's fumble at the Alabama 3-yard line with the score knotted at 34. On second down, tailback Jacob Hester scored from a yard out and Colt David's extra point made it 41-34 with 1:26 to play, and No. 3 LSU (8-1) held on to take over first place in the Southeastern Conference West at 5-1.

No. 17 Alabama (6-3, 4-2) led 27-17 in the third quarter. When the Crimson Tide took a 34-27 lead with 7:33 remaining on a 61-yard punt return by Javier Arenas, it looked like LSU fans' worst nightmare was coming true with their hated Saban as Satan and the Tigers in hell. But somehow, the Tigers came through one more time to keep their BCS national championship hopes alive.

"Thank God it's over," said LSU athletic director Skip Bertman, who replaced the NFL-bound Saban with Miles in 2005, as he exited the press box.

"Whew, that's a true freshman," Miles said of Jones, who wheeled Wilson around on the sack just before the ball popped out. "He came over to us from baseball practice. Boy, he's been invaluable. He made a great play

on that knockout."

Jones, a 13th-round pick of the Houston Astros, chose LSU over Major League Baseball just as football practice was beginning last August. He has his home run now.

"It was a big-play opportunity," Jones said. "I kind of slugged him and shook the ball loose. I was so excited I didn't know what to think."

Alabama, which fought off a 17-3 deficit in the second quarter to take a 20-17 halftime lead, was not done, though. Wilson fought off what would have been an eighth sack by the Tigers and scrambled for a 23-yard gain to the LSU 49 with just over a minute to play. Three straight incompletions followed. Then on fourth-and-10 with 51 seconds to play, Wilson apparently threw complete to wide receiver Keith Brown for a first down. But safety Craig Steltz lowered his shoulder on Brown, who dropped the ball incomplete.

LSU took over and ran out the clock, beating its former coach who still has nearly 30 signees on the current roster.

"It was good to get this game behind us and let coach Miles know that this is his team," said senior quarterback and Saban signee Matt Flynn.

Flynn completed 24 of 44 passes for 353 yards and three touchdowns. He fought off three second-quarter interceptions to deliver LSU its second consecutive come-from-behind victory. Two of the interceptions led to 10 Alabama points. True freshman Kareem Jackson, a Saban signee, returned one of the interceptions 51 yards to set up a 29-yard touchdown pass by Wilson to Brown, giving the Tide a 20-17 lead just before halftime.

LSU faced defeat and Saban square in the face with

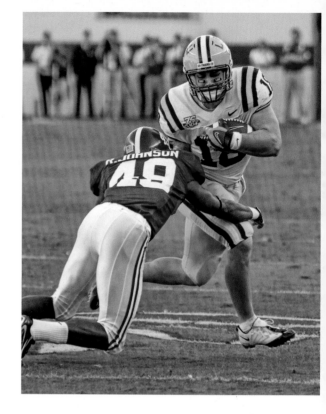

Above: LSU's Jacob Hester (18) tries to break a tackle from Alabama's Rashad Johnson (49). *Photo by Tim Eddington/Special to The Times*

Opposite: LSU's Early Doucet (9) heads up field after making a catch. *Photo by Tim Eddington/Special to The Times*

2:58 remaining in the game and trailing 34-27 as it lined up for a fourth-and-4 from the Tide 32-yard line. Flynn completed a short pass to wide receiver Early Doucet, who shook off one tackler, reversed his field and scored with 2:49 to play. Flynn fielded a high snap over his far shoulder on the extra point snap, and David made it for a 34-34 tie.

"It was a Z choice route," Doucet said. "I knew once I caught it I had a chance to score because the guy who had an angle on me was going too hard. I knew I could cut back on him, and I did and was able to get in the end zone."

Doucet, a Saban signee, caught five passes for 67 yards and two touchdowns.

"This was a great win for coach Miles," Doucet said. "He was getting criticized for playing with coach Saban's players. Some people were down on him. But coach Miles is a great coach. I'm happy to be playing for him."

LSU overcame a season-high 14 penalties for 130 yards, including several personal fouls, and the three interceptions.

"I've got to tell you we kept hanging in there, kept fighting, kept struggling," Miles said. "I've never seen so many mistakes by a team in a game or a season. But I enjoyed the resolve of our team. I thought Alabama played a damn good football game. I credit Nick Saban. He's done a damn good job with that team." ∎

Left: LSU's Glenn Dorsey (72) puts pressure on Alabama quarterback John Parker Wilson. *Photo by Tim Eddington/Special to The Times*

#3 LSU vs. #17 Alabama
November 3, 2007 | Tuscaloosa, AL

SCORING SUMMARY

Team	1st	2nd	3rd	4th	End
LSU	10	7	7	17	41
Alabama	3	17	7	7	34

First quarter
UA – Leigh Tiffin 36 field goal 12:30
LSU – Colt David 43 field goal 6:05
LSU – Early Doucet 10 pass from Matt Flynn (David kick) 4:30

Second quarter
LSU – Jacob Hester 1 run (David kick) 14:56
UA – DJ Hall 67 pass from John Parker Wilson (Tiffin kick) 11:03
UA – Tiffin 21 field goal 6:12
UA – Keith Brown 29 pass from Wilson (Tiffin kick) :46

Third quarter
UA – Brown 14 pass from Wilson (Tiffin kick) 1:19
LSU – Demetrius Byrd 61 pass from Flynn (David kick) :20

Fourth quarter
LSU – David 49 field goal 11:21
UA – Javier Arenas 61 punt return (Tiffin kick) 7:33
LSU – Early Doucet 32 pass from Flynn (David kick) 2:49
LSU – Hester 1 run (David kick) 1:26

TEAM STATS	LSU	UA
First Downs	21	20
Rush-Pass-Penalty	6-15-0	2-12-6
Rushes-Yards	34-87	33-20
Passing Yards	388	234
Com-Att-Int	25-46-3	14-40-1
Total Plays	80	73
Total Yards	475	254
Avg. Gain Per Play	5.9	3.5
Fumbles: No.-Lost	1-0	2-1
Penalties: No.-Yards	14-130	2-15
Punts-Avg	6-46.0	8-33.4
Punt Returns: No.-Yards	3-18	3-69
Kickoff Returns: No.-Yards	7-106	8-168
Interceptions: No.-Yards	1-18	3-53
Possession Time	33:17	26:43
Third-Down Conv.	6-16	4-17
Fourth-Down Conv.	1-1	0-1
Sacks By: No.-Yards	7-53	3-19

INDIVIDUAL STATS: LSU

Rushing	No	Yds	TD	Lg
Jacob Hester	16	47	2	9
Keiland Williams	3	24	0	15
Matt Flynn	10	19	0	12
Trindon Holliday	1	2	0	2
Richard Murphy	1	0	0	0
Charles Scott	1	-1	0	0

Passing	Att	Com	Int	Yds	TD	Lg
Matt Flynn	44	24	3	353	3	61

Receiving	No.	Yds	TD	Lg
Demetrius Byrd	6	114	1	61
Early Doucet	5	67	2	32
Jacob Hester	5	33	0	18
Brandon LaFell	4	43	0	19
Richard Dickson	3	55	0	35
Matt Flynn	1	35	0	35
Terrance Toliver	1	11	0	11

Punting	No.	Yds	Avg	Lg
Patrick Fisher	6	276	46.0	52

INDIVIDUAL STATS: Alabama

Rushing	No	Yds	TD	Lg
Jonathan Lowe	10	31	0	8
Terry Grant	13	23	0	5
DJ Hall	1	0	0	0
John Parker Wilson	9	-34	0	23

Passing	Att	Com	Int	Yds	TD	Lg
John Parker Wilson	40	14	1	234	3	67

Receiving	No.	Yds	TD	Lg
Matt Caddell	3	55	0	32
Terry Grant	3	29	0	15
DJ Hall	2	76	1	67
Keith Brown	2	43	2	29
Nick Walker	2	25	0	15
Mike McCoy	1	4	0	4
Jonathan Lowe	1	2	0	2

Punting	No.	Yds	Avg	Lg
P.J. Fitzgerald	8	267	33.4	37

Hester's dive preserves LSU's march

By Roy Lang III | The Times

With two hands locked around the ball as if the 3 feet of grass he needed to traverse meant the world, Shreveport's Jacob Hester leapt from the turf that had been so nasty to his team all night and landed safely on the next step in LSU's march toward the ultimate goal.

Using the strength and security of one of the country's most reliable runners and the grace of a frolicking dolphin, Hester dove into the end zone with 1:26 remaining. The score capped a stunning LSU comeback and 41-34 victory over the Crimson Tide.

On an evening marked by gaffes not reflective of a national title contender, the Tigers were lucky to be handed one more chance to keep their SEC and national championship dreams alive.

To a man, the LSU Tigers had no doubt the ball needed to be in the hands of the most reliable guy dressed in visitors' white.

"When we need those yards and we need ball security, I don't think there's any question who we're giving the ball to," said LSU quarterback Matt Flynn, who was bailed out by his teammate after his three consecutive interceptions revived the Crimson Tide in the second quarter.

Dubbed "Stubby Legs" by Nick Saban, Hester, who finished with 47 yards and two touchdowns on 16 carries, dashed his former head coach's bid for a stunning upset. After one of his patented pushes up the middle, Hester showed some style and executed an unusual — for him — 1-yard dive over the Alabama defensive line.

Himself a culprit of one of the Tigers' seemingly infinite mistakes, Hester secured the pigskin and cured a rash of carelessness.

"Hester is a tough, hard-nosed guy," LSU head coach Les Miles said. "We like his ball security and the toughness with which he runs. We knew we were giving it to a seasoned guy."

And a determined guy.

Hester not only wanted to bring Miles — who he feels is underappreciated — a victory, he wanted to rectify his mistake.

Hester helped put Alabama in prime scoring position late in the first half when he was called for a personal foul after ran down cornerback Kareem Jackson following Flynn's third interception.

"Emotions were definitely high," Hester said. "I went to tackle a guy on the Alabama sideline after the interception and all I saw was 20 Crimson jerseys. I was trying to get out of there as fast as I could. We definitely let the emotions get the best of us."

Alabama scored two plays later to take a 20-17 halftime lead.

LSU committed a season-high 14 penalties for 130 yards Saturday and turned the ball over three times. Alabama played a relatively flawless game (two penalties for 15 yards and one turnover) until the game's waning moments.

As true freshman safety Chad Jones sacked Alabama quarterback John Parker Wilson and spun him around inside the Crimson Tide 10, the ball came loose and LSU safety Curtis Taylor pounced on it at the 3 with 1:39 left.

That's when LSU turned to its best — and only appropriate — option.

"We had three plays called and two of them go to Jacob Hester," LSU offensive coordinator Gary Crowton said. "Maybe we'll go to the third one next time." ■

Opposite top: LSU tight end Richard Dickson (82) makes a catch against Alabama in the Tigers' 41-34 win.
Photo by Tim Eddington/Special to The Times

Opposite bottom: LSU quarterback Matt Flynn (15) throws a pass against Alabama during the Tigers' win over the Crimson Tide.
Photo by Tim Eddington/Special to The Times

Left: LSU quarterback Matt Flynn (15) tries to run past Alabama's Rashad Johnson. *Photo by Tim Eddington/Special to The Times*

Bottom left: The LSU band plays during the Tigers' 41-34 win over Alabama. *Photo by Tim Eddington/Special to The Times*

Bottom right: LSU coach Les Miles talks to his team during the Tigers' win over Alabama. *Photo by Tim Eddington/Special to The Times*

Opposite left: LSU wide receiver Demetrius Byrd (2) races to the end zone for a touchdown against Alabama.
Photo by Tim Eddington/Special to The Times

Opposite top: LSU wide receiver Early Doucet (9) runs after making a catch against the Alabama defense.
Photo by Tim Eddington/Special to The Times

Opposite bottom: LSU cornerback Jai Eugene (4) celebrates during his team's win over Alabama.
Photo by Tim Eddington/Special to The Times

Left: LSU wide receivers Brandon LaFell (1) and Early Doucet (9) celebrate during LSU's 41-34 victory over Alabama.
Photo by Tim Eddington/Special to The Times

Louisiana Tech

Above: LSU fans show their spirit. *Photo by Val Horvath/The Times*

Left: LSU's Terrance Toliver (80) runs down field. *Photo by Val Horvath/The Times*

Tigers top Tech to move back to No. 1

By Glenn Guilbeau | Louisiana Gannett News

LSU moved back to No. 1 after previous No. 1 Ohio State lost to Illinois and LSU defeated Louisiana Tech, 58-10.

Alabama, Nick Saban and Auburn also lost, meaning LSU clinched a berth in the Southeastern Conference Championship Game before it took the field Saturday night.

Happy 54th birthday, Les Miles.

"All in all, it was a nice night," the LSU coach said. "Yeah! how about the fans singing, 'Happy Birthday.'"

Going into the game, LSU was No. 2 in the Bowl Championship Series rankings that decide the combatants in the Jan. 7 national championship game in New Orleans.

"Hopefully, if we keep executing, I don't think anyone can beat us," said tight end Richard Dickson, who

---

Top: LSU's Matt Flynn passes against the Louisiana Tech defense. *Photo by Val Horvath/The Times*

Bottom: The LSU band prepares for its show.
Photo by Val Horvath/The Times

Far right: LSU's cheerleaders stand at attention.
Photo by Val Horvath/The Times

caught one of three touchdown passes by quarterback Matt Flynn.

LSU piled up 595 yards of offense in beating Tech in front of 92,512 at Tiger Stadium as Flynn threw for 237 and tailback Jacob Hester rushed for 115 with an 87-yard touchdown run.

"It feels nice," said Flynn, who completed 14 of 26 passes with a 71-yard touchdown pass to Terrance Toliver, a 37-yard touchdown to Brandon LaFell and a 14 yarder to Dickson. "We know we're going to the SEC Championship Game. We could be No. 1, but we've got to keep playing like we're playing. It is what it is. It's nice to know we're in control of our own destiny for the national championship game."

The best Mississippi State or either Alabama or Auburn can finish in the West is 5-3. The Tigers are 5-1 in the West and could lose their remaining two league games and still win the division because they have tie-breaker victories over State, Alabama and Auburn. LSU will play the SEC East champion on Dec. 1 in Atlanta in its fourth SEC Championship Game in seven years.

The Tigers did not look like world — or nation — beaters in the early going as Tech drew within 10-7 in the opening moments of the second quarter on a 37-yard touchdown pass from quarterback Zac Champion to Brian Jackson. Tech, a 3-3 team in the Western Athletic Conference that fell to 4-6 overall, had LSU outgained 88 yards to 55 despite trailing 10-0 after the first quarter.

The Tigers began to look like a No. 1 when Flynn connected with Toliver on the 71-yard score for a touchdown and 20-7 lead with 8:12 to go before halftime. Flynn later found LaFell, who turned a short pass into a 37-yard touchdown and 27-7 lead with 56 seconds remaining before halftime.

LSU poured it on in the second half with precision. First Colt David kicked his third field goal of the night and a school-record tying 19th on the season from 28 yards away for a 30-7 lead at the 12:17 mark. David Browndyke also kicked 19 field goals in 1988.

After three plays and a punt by Tech, LSU's Hester popped up the middle for an 87-yard touchdown and 37-7 lead with 10:15 to play in the third period. It was the fifth-longest rushing touchdown in LSU history and the longest since Justin Vincent also had an 87-yard touchdown run in the win over Georgia in the 2003 SEC Championship Game.

Just two minutes and 13 seconds later after another three-and-out by Tech, Flynn found Dickson for a 14-yard touchdown and 44-7 advantage.

"I noticed that they were trying to be insulting and run up the score on us," Tech safety Antonio Baker said. "I didn't pay any attention to that."

Tech cut that margin to 44-10 on a 38-yard field goal by Danny Horwedel early in the fourth quarter.

Then came the style points. LSU drove 72 yards in six plays for a touchdown and 51-10 lead with 9:20 remaining in the game as tailback Trindon Holliday darted and cut his way for a 16-yard touchdown run. Tailback Richard Murphy bolted 53 yards to the Tech 10 to set up the score.

Then it was backup quarterback Ryan Perrilloux's turn. Perrilloux, in his first action since a suspension nearly two weeks ago, scrambled and unleashed a 35-yard pass to Toliver to the 2-yard line. One play later, Perrilloux found tight end Mit Cole for the 2-yard touchdown and 58-10 lead with 4:42 to play.

LSU took a 7-0 lead with just over two minutes elapsed in the first quarter on a 1-yard touchdown run by Flynn. Champion fumbled on Tech's second play of the game, and LSU outside linebacker Ali Highsmith recovered at the Bulldogs' 24-yard line. An end around by Toliver gained 20 yards to the 1-yard line.

David made it 10-0 with his first field goal of the night from 31 yards out with 3:35 to play in the first quarter.

"We enjoy the position of number one," Miles said. "But it's like being number one before number one counts."

At the moment, LSU's players were more concerned about number 54.

"We were going to do something for his birthday before the game," Hester said. "But he was in a serious mode." ∎

LSU starts slow, finishes like a (SEC) champ

By Teddy Allen | The Times

In a college football season crazy as the inside of grandma's handbag, Saturday night in Tiger Stadium was more of the same.

LSU has done its part in making the 2007 season a constant of wind shifts, flash floods and changing undercurrents, a rollercoaster minus the coasting part. Even as the No. 2-ranked team in the Bowl Championship Series and a 35-point favorite — and a 58-10 winner — against Louisiana Tech, the Tigers kept fans wondering for the better part of the first half: Are we watching this year's best team?

They had their answer, though not technically, a couple of hours before the 7 p.m. kickoff. The BCS' No. 1 team, Ohio State, had fallen in the late afternoon to Illinois. SEC West challengers Auburn and Alabama had each lost in Saturday's twilight.

Hello, five-touchdown underdog Tech. Hello, No. 1 BCS ranking. Hello, SEC West title.

You should have been able to hear the lip-smackin' and jaw-chompin' coming from the home team locker room during pregame ankle taping. Shoot, even before

Left: LSU's Lazarius Levingston (95) works against the Louisiana Tech offensive line. *Photo by Val Horvath/The Times*

half the crowd of 92,000-plus had found its seat, LSU had already earned a spot in the Dec. 1 SEC Championship Game in Atlanta.

So with everything going its way, the skids greased and a fortunate 3-1 in nailbiters coming out of the most wacky month of games in Tiger history, LSU had opened for it a window of opportunity the size of the Atchafalya Basin — and crawled through it.

The final score shouldn't fool you. LSU's athletic budget is a cool $70 million. Tech's is $10 million. Judged by the final score, a single point in a game of tackle football these days is $1.5 million, give or take.

The game was never in doubt. But home team fans — about a third of them left after the third quarter — had trouble getting into it. So did home team players.

Two early Tech turnovers equaled 10 Tigers points. The first was a fumble on Tech's second play from scrimmage on its own 24 — not the way you want to start the game on the road — and then the second turnover came on a deep snap "team fumble" as the ball's hiker, Thomas Graham, hiked the ball into his own leg. I had never seen this before but would imagine that it's not generally a good thing for the punt team. It wasn't here: Jacob Hester, who plays on the punt coverage team for LSU when he's not playing everywhere else, recovered at the Tech 18; his team managed a field goal.

But a quick Bulldogs two-step later — an interception and a TD pass — and Tech trailed only 10-7 with 13:14 left in the first half.

Neither team's momentum was helped by football fate on this night. The game clock kept going out. Then the play clock. There was another of those interminable "play under review" deals. And midway though the second quarter, line judge Paul Petrisko was smashed on a sweep and was last seen leaving, by way of gurney and Acadian AmbulanceServices, with a compound fracture in his shin.

Ouch.

Tech was hurt just as badly two plays later when LSU showed its first first-class flash of the night, a 71-yard touchdown pass from Matt Flynn to Terrance Toliver and a 20-7 lead.

Flynn to a sideline-walking Brandon LaFell was good for a 37-yard TD and a 27-7 LSU halftime lead, but even that seemed less than satisfying for a fairly docile Tiger Stadium crowd. Tech's Zac Champion was picked off in the end zone with 11 seconds left in the half, helping the Tigers dodge what would have been an unseemly cushion of just 10 points.

Instead, that interception meant LSU was just getting warmed up. LSU outscored Tech 31-3 in the second half.

Its own worst enemy for the past month, LSU had averaged two turnovers and nine penalties for 80 yards per game its last four outings. The Tigers turned it over two times and were penalized eight times for 60 yards against the Bulldogs, who turned it over a coffin-nailing five times.

Finally, the timing of Tech's scheduling of LSU has not been the greatest. In the most recent meeting between the two, Tech lost to LSU, 49-10. That was in 2003. LSU won the national championship two months later. ■

Louisiana Tech vs. #2 LSU
November 10, 2007 | Baton Rouge, LA

SCORING SUMMARY

Team	1st	2nd	3rd	4th	End
Louisiana Tech	0	7	0	3	10
LSU	10	17	17	14	58

First quarter
LSU – Matt Flynn 1 run (Colt David kick) 12:51
LSU – David 31 field goal 3:35

Second quarter
LT – Brian Jackson 37 pass from Zac Champion (Danny Horwedel kick) 13:14
LSU – David 44 field goal 10:40
LSU – Terrance Toliver 71 pass from Matt Flynn (David kick) 8:12
LSU – Brandon LaFell 37 pass from Flynn (David kick) :56

Third quarter
LSU – David 28 field goal 12:17
LSU – Jacob Hester 87 run (David kick) 10:15
LSU – Richard Dickson 14 pass from Flynn (David kick) 8:02

Fourth quarter
LT – Horwedel 38 field goal 13:09
LSU – Trindon Holliday 15 run (David kick) 9:20
LSU – Mit Cole 2 pass from Ryan Perrilloux (David kick) 4:42

TEAM STATS

	LT	LSU
First Downs	15	22
Rush-Pass-Penalty	5-9-1	10-10-2
Rushes-Yards	35-67	40-321
Passing Yards	189	274
Com-Att-Int	20-39-2	16-30-2
Total Plays	74	70
Total Yards	256	595
Avg. Gain Per Play	3.5	8.5
Fumbles: No.-Lost	3-3	0-0
Penalties: No.-Yards	6-75	8-60
Punts-Avg	7-43.1	3.42.7
Punt Returns: No.-Yards	1-5	3-14
Kickoff Returns: No.-Yards	10-318	2-38
Interceptions: No.-Yards	2-10	2-33
Fumble Returns: No-Yards	0-0	0-0
Possession Time	31:14	28:46
Third-Down Conv.	2-16	4-12
Fourth-Down Conv.	1-5	0-1
Sacks By: No.-Yards	2-16	2-12

INDIVIDUAL STATS: Louisiana Tech

Rushing

	No.	Yds	TD	Lg
Patrick Jackson	9	42	0	13
William Griffin	8	20	0	9
Zac Champion	8	7	0	7
Chris Keagle	1	2	0	2
Daniel Porter	8	-1	0	3

Passing

	Att	Cmp	Int	Yds	TD	Lg
Zac Champion	39	20	2	189	1	37

Receiving

	No.	Yds	TD	Lg
Dustin Mitchell	5	29	0	14
William Griffin	3	20	0	12
Joe Anderson	3	13	0	6
Shane Womack	2	26	0	15
Anthony Harrison	2	24	0	24
Patrick Jackson	2	10	0	6
Brian Jackson	1	37	1	37
Phillip Livas	1	15	0	15
Philip Beck	1	15	0	15

Punting

	No.	Yds	Avg	Lg
Chris Keagle	7	302	43.1	56

INDIVIDUAL STATS: LSU

Rushing

	No.	Yds	TD	Lg
Jacob Hester	11	115	1	87
Richard Murphy	3	62	0	53
Trindon Holliday	5	45	1	15
Shawn Jordan	4	32	0	15
Keiland Williams	4	29	0	15
Terrance Toliver	1	20	0	20
Charles Scott	5	13	0	12
Matt Flynn	4	9	1	9
Ryan Perrilloux	2	-3	0	7

Passing

	Att	Cmp	Int	Yds	TD	Lg
Matt Flynn	26	14	2	237	3	71
Ryan Perrilloux	4	2	0	37	1	35

Receiving

	No.	Yds.	TD	Lg
Brandon LaFell	5	80	1	37
Terrance Toliver	3	119	1	71
Early Doucet	3	22	0	15
Richard Dickson	2	30	1	16
Demetrius Byrd	2	21	0	12
Mit Cole	1	2	1	2

Punting

	No.	Yds	Avg	Lg
Patrick Fisher	3	128	42.7	55

Above: LSU's Matt Flynn (15) scrambles against Louisiana Tech. *Photo by Val Horvath/The Times*

Opposite: LSU's Shawn Jordan makes a run during a game against Louisiana Tech at Tiger Stadium in Baton Rouge. *Photo by Val Horvath/The Times*

Ole Miss

Above: Ole Miss fans cheer on their team against LSU. *Photo by Ryan Moore/The Clarion-Ledger*

Left: LSU running back Jacob Hester (18) looks for yardage inside against Ole Miss.
Photo by Ryan Moore/The Clarion-Ledger

LSU defeats Ole Miss to clinch SEC West outright

By Glenn Guilbeau | Louisiana Gannett News

It was a pretty enough final score, but No. 1 LSU often played Saturday like it needs a couple more trips to the beauty parlor before its big night.

Struggling Ole Miss, which limped in winless in the Southeastern Conference, outgained the Tigers 466 yards to 396 and drew within 10 twice in the final quarter before falling 41-24 in front of 61,118 at Vaught-Hemingway Stadium.

"This is our 10th victory and we are outright SEC West division champions," LSU coach Les Miles said. "Great position to be in. I can also tell you we can play a little bit better."

The Tigers (10-1) collected double-digit victories for a record third straight season under the third-year coach and captured the school's first unshared SEC West title in improving to 6-1 in the West.

"It's a little surprising we didn't close the game out earlier with our defense," Miles said.

LSU's defense had not allowed that many yards since Arizona State put up 560 in losing 35-31 in Miles' first game as LSU's coach in 2005.

But LSU did not have a lot of offense in the early going either. The Tigers led the Rebels (3-8, 0-7 SEC) by just 14-7 at halftime, thanks to a 98-yard kickoff return for a touchdown by Trindon Holliday with 3:04 to play in the first quarter. That followed a 44-yard punt return by Bastrop's Marshay Green that tied the game 7-7 seconds before.

Ole Miss was threatening to tie the game at 14 before half, but safety Craig Steltz intercepted quarterback Seth Adams in the end zone with 25 seconds left. The Rebels also had a chance for a touchdown in the first quarter before the punt return with a first-and-goal at the 2 following a 37-yard kickoff return by Mike Wallace and a short drive.

But tailback BenJarvus Green-Ellis fumbled when middle linebacker Jacob Cutrera hit him, and linebacker Luke Sanders recovered.

"There were some obvious turning points," Ole Miss coach Ed Orgeron said. "We made some plays, but we didn't get it done."

LSU's only other score in the first half came on its first possession of the game as it went 98 yards in 11 near-flawless plays in which it looked like it was ready to rout the 19-point spread. Jacob Hester gained 14 yards on the first three carries. Quarterback Matt Flynn found receiver Demetrius Byrd for 11 and hit tailback Richard Murphy in the flat for a 21-yard catch and run. Keiland Williams spelled Hester with a 21-yard run. Holliday made an appearance for 7 yards. Flynn hit Early Doucet for 10 and later scored on the option from 5 yards out for the 7-0 lead with 7:37 to play.

It looked like a clinic. Then it stopped.

"I think as an offense we did what was necessary to win the game," said Flynn, who was efficient in completing 17 of 25 passes for 168 yards and no interceptions.

"When we need to, we do it," said Doucet, who led all receivers with eight catches for 58 yards. "Eventually, it'll get to a point where we have all points of our game clicking all the time."

The next time the offense figured it needed it was with the opening kickoff of the third quarter. The Tigers went 54 yards in 10 plays with Williams scoring on a 10-yard run for a 21-7 lead. LSU went up 27-10 on a

Top: Ole Miss wide receiver Dexter McCluster tries to slip away from LSU's Harry Coleman as other defenders close in.
Photo by Ryan Moore/The Clarion-Ledger

Above: LSU and Ole Miss fans get ready for the game.
Photo by Ryan Moore/The Clarion-Ledger

pair of field goals by Colt David of 48 and 43 yards that gave him the school record of 21 in a season. But Ole Miss wouldn't go away.

Almost forgotten Rebels' quarterback Brent Schaeffer, who had played in only four games before Saturday, threw for a career-high 208 yards on 13-of-28 passing and rushed eight times for 94 yards. He scrambled for a 38-yard touchdown to cut LSU's lead to 27-17 with 9:11 to play and threw a 33-yard touchdown pass to Shay Hodge with 2:54 to play to get the Rebels within 34-24.

"He's a shifty guy," Cutrera said. "We let him get outside. It happened a few times. We played so-so, definitely not our best. We have to do better."

LSU had gone up 34-17 on a 2-yard run by Hester

after Steltz set up the Tigers at the Ole Miss 20 with a 42-yard return of his second interception and sixth of the season. Tailback Charles Scott, who gained 66 yards on three carries, put LSU up 41-24 on a 29-yard touchdown run through a tiring Rebels defense with 2:15 to play. Hester finished with 66 yards on 13 carries with a 17-yard run before Scott's touchdown.

"In a game like that, you try not to make mistakes," Flynn said. "When we needed to make plays toward the end, we did. That's been us all year. They played well. They came out fired up. But we kept grinding and grinding. It probably wasn't the prettiest day on offense today, but it was what needed to be done. We'll take it. It worked. We're still in control of our own destiny." ■

LSU's Miles is a man of many hats

By Bob Heist | The Daily Advertiser

Fear The Hat?

The rest of the country might, but not Les Miles. And add in the players on the LSU football coach's team, too.

Across the board, they all chuckled at the suggestion.

"No comment," senior defensive end Kirston Pittman said. "But 'Fear The Hat' — that's good; crazy, but good."

If you haven't figured it out yet, "The Hat" is Miles, an affectionate nickname growing legs across Tiger Nation for his trademark baseball cap worn on game day. And the reference really does seem apropos, because Miles has certainly worn plenty of them this season for top-ranked LSU.

Let's count the ways:

• Gambler. Rolling the dice on five successful fourth-down calls that willed the Tigers past Florida.

• Trickster. The fake field goal against South Carolina that allowed kicker Colt David to run 15 yards for a touchdown and a 21-7 lead against the Ol' Ball Coach.

• Psychiatrist. The nation's 19th-ranked offense has been among the worst with dropped passes. And just when you're ready to give up on them, culprit Demetrius Byrd catches the game-winning pass with one second to play against Auburn and then grabs six balls for a career-best 144 yards and a key 61-yard score at Alabama.

• Bail bondsman. Miles has had numerous players since last spring involved in legal issues, specifically backup quarterback Ryan Perrilloux. Somehow, that

Above: Ole Miss quarterback Brent Schaeffer runs for a first down against the LSU Tigers. *Photo by Ryan Moore/The Clarion-Ledger*

Left: LSU head coach Les Miles argues a call with an official.
Photo by Ryan Moore/The Clarion-Ledger

Opposite: Ole Miss running back BenJarvus Green-Ellis watches the ball after he fumbled on the 2-yard line.
Photo by Ryan Moore/The Clarion-Ledger

—- plus other dismissals and suspensions — has never become a distraction.

• Choo-Choo Charlie. He found a way to keep LSU's season on track with the triple-overtime loss at Kentucky falling right after the epic Florida win and right before crucial SEC West games against Auburn and 'Bama.

• Dunce. We might as well fess up to the fact that the Tigers have at times been extremely disorganized with substitutions, are average at best at covering kicks, and are the most penalized team in the Southeastern Conference. Miles says the team will address those areas every week, but hey, if at first you don't succeed ...

There are several reasons this equal parts uneven and eventful season has been so interesting in Baton Rouge, and Miles is certainly near the top of the list.

Since 1959, no LSU team had ever been ranked No. 1 in-season until this year. Following Sunday's vote, this is the Tigers' second go-round. And it is for Miles, too.

Above: Ole Miss Rebel Marshay Green heads for the sideline to gain yards on a punt return. Green returned the ball 44 yards for a touchdown. *Photo by Ryan Moore/The Clarion-Ledger*

Top right: Ole Miss quarterback Brent Schaeffer runs for a first down as LSU Tiger Chevis Jackson attempt to tackle.
Photo by Ryan Moore/The Clarion-Ledger

Remember, while his 31-5 record is the best start to a coaching tenure with the program, Miles is in unchartered waters.

He never played on a Michigan team that was ranked No. 1 in the mid-70's. As an assistant at Michigan and Colorado, he never coached on a staff with a top-ranked team. He spent three seasons as an assistant with average Dallas Cowboys teams. His best record in four seasons as the head coach at Oklahoma State before coming to the bayou was 9-4 in 2003.

Has Miles made mistakes? Would Paris Hilton sweat at a spelling bee?

The guy's human — flawed and brilliant at the same time. And his players love him. That's obvious. And you won't find that in a box score.

"You don't get anywhere like this without a great leader," senior All-American Glenn Dorsey said, "and that's Coach Miles. The guy's tremendous."

"I've said it before, he's a great father figure," Pittman said. "He's a gambler and a risk-taker on the field, and there have been some things off the field that have happened that go against what we believe in and what we stand for. They could have jeopardized our season, but he didn't allow us to let that happen.

"He's the conductor of the train, he's the captain of the ship ..."

No, he's The Hat.

"I have no reason to fear the hat," Miles deadpanned. "I put it on my head every day."

The guy's priceless. ■

#1 LSU vs. Ole Miss
November 17, 2007 | Oxford, MS

SCORING SUMMARY

Team	1st	2nd	3rd	4th	End
LSU	14	0	10	17	41
Ole Miss	7	0	3	14	24

First quarter
LSU – Matt Flynn 5 run (Colt David kick) 7:37
UM – Marshay Green 44 punt return (Joshua Shene kick) 3:18
LSU – Trindon Holliday 98 kickoff return (David kick) 3:04

Third quarter
LSU – Keiland Williams 10 run (David kick) 10:10
UM – Shene 23 field goal 6:51
LSU – David 48 field goal 4:23

Fourth quarter
LSU – David 43 field goal 11:36
UM – Brent Schaeffer 38 run (Shene kick) 9:11
LSU – Jacob Hester 2 run (David kick) 3:44
UM – Shay Hodge 33 pass from Scheaffer (Shene kick) 2:54
LSU – Charles Scott 29 run (David kick) 2:15

TEAM STATS

	LSU	UM
First Downs	21	25
Rush-Pass-Penalty	12-9-0	11-11-3
Rushes-Yards	40-228	28-201
Passing Yards	168	265
Com-Att-Int	17-25-0	17-39-3
Total Plays	65	67
Total Yards	396	466
Avg. Gain Per Play	6.1	7.0
Fumbles: No.-Lost	0-0	1-1
Penalties: No.-Yards	9-66	8-74
Punts-Avg.	4-41.5	4-40.0
Punt Returns: No.-Yards	0-0	2-49
Kickoff Returns: No.-Yards	4-127	7-133
Interceptions: No.-Yards	3-42	0-0
Possession Time	30:56	29:04
Third-Down Conv.	4-11	5-10
Fourth-Down Conv.	1-1	0-0
Sacks By: No.-Yards	1-8	3-25

INDIVIDUAL STATS: LSU

Rushing	No	Yds	TD	Lg
Charles Scott	3	66	1	29
Jacob Hester	13	65	1	17
Keiland Williams	5	41	1	21
Trindon Holliday	4	25	0	10
Richard Murphy	3	17	0	13
Matt Flynn	12	14	1	9

INDIVIDUAL STATS: LSU

Passing	Att	Com	Int	Yds	TD	Lg
Matt Flynn	25	17	0	168	0	21

Receiving	No.	Yds	TD	Lg
Early Doucet	8	58	0	12
Brandon LaFell	3	19	0	11
Keiland Williams	2	38	0	20
Richard Murphy	1	21	0	21
Jacob Hester	1	14	0	14
Demetrius Byrd	1	11	0	11
Charles Scott	1	7	0	7

Punting	No.	Yds	Avg	Lg
Patrick Fisher	4	166	41.5	56

INDIVIDUAL STATS: Ole Miss

Rushing	No	Yds	TD	Lg
Brent Schaeffer	8	94	1	38
BenJarvus Green-Ellis	12	53	0	16
Dexter McCluster	2	38	0	29
Bruce Hall	4	15	0	7
Seth Adams	2	1	0	4

Passing	Att	Com	Int	Yds	TD	Lg
Brent Schaeffer	28	13	2	208	1	39
Seth Adams	11	4	1	57	0	21

Receiving	No.	Yds	TD	Lg
Dexter McCluster	5	73	0	24
Shay Hodge	4	90	1	39
Marshay Green	3	17	0	13
Jason Cook	2	14	0	14
Bruce Hall	1	35	0	35
Robert Hough	1	21	0	21
Michael Hicks	1	15	0	15

Punting	No.	Yds	Avg	Lg
Justin Sparks	4	160	40.0	43

Above: Ole Miss running back BenJarvus Green-Ellis uses a block to his advantage to gain yards against the LSU Tigers. *Photo by Ryan Moore/The Clarion-Ledger*

Left: Ole Miss quarterback Seth Adams tries to gain yards. *Photo by Ryan Moore/The Clarion-Ledger*

Holliday, LSU return game break through

By Roy Lang III | The Times

Trindon Holliday played simultaneous roles in, "Anything You Can Do I Can Do Better" and "Buzz Kill" on Saturday at Vaught-Hemingway Stadium.

Moments after this quaint arena exploded in joy due to a punt return for a touchdown by the homestanding Ole Miss Rebels, LSU's diminutive special threat countered big time.

Holliday's 98-yard romp on the ensuing kickoff late in the first quarter put the Tigers— ranked 11th of 12 teams in the SEC and 110th of 119 teams in the country in kickoff returns — ahead for good.

"It was Trindon saying, 'No, we're going to keep that one-touchdown lead,'" LSU head coach Les Miles said after his team's 41-24 victory. "It was big, just what we needed."

Fourteen seconds — that's all Rebels and their fans were able to celebrate following Marshay Green's 44-yard punt return late in the first quarter, which pulled Ole Miss into a 7-7 tie.

Holliday, a track champion, took the kick at the right hash, broke through the initial pursuit and comically outran the Rebels' kicker.

"The momentum was shifted to them. The coaches told us to watch the ball off the tee and make a big play," Holliday said. "It was on my shoulders to make a big

play. I just ran behind my wedge, saw a crease and just hit it."

Monday, during his news conference, Miles predicted a huge play from his special teams. Most probably chalked it up to a coach being a bit biased as the Tigers ranked 11th out of 12 (Mississippi State is last) Southeastern Conference teams and 110th out of 119 FBS (formerly Division I-A) teams in kickoff returns (18.2 yards per) heading into Saturday.

"Our return teams are playing better," Miles said. "It was just a matter of time before that guy got loose, as you can see. If he gets just a little bit of space, it's a lot of space."

As he often does, Miles took a few moments to revel in the spectacular play.

"It's surely entertaining isn't it? Great fun," the enthusiastic head coach said.

The touchdown more than doubled LSU's longest kick return for the 2007 season (a 44-yarder by Holliday (at Kentucky, Oct. 13). It marked the first score on a kickoff since Holliday's 92-yard jaunt at Arkansas last season.

Only four kickoff returns in LSU history were longer. Eric Martin (1981 vs. Kentucky) and Sammy Grezaffi (1967 vs. Tennessee) are tied for the LSU record with 100-yard kickoff returns.

"That's the easiest drive for an offense," LSU quarterback Matt Flynn said. ■

Right: LSU Tiger Charles Scott makes his way down the sideline to the end zone for a touchdown. *Photo by Ryan Moore/The Clarion-Ledger*

Opposite top: Ole Miss running back BenJarvus Green-Ellis carries the ball for a first down as LSU defenders close in. *Photo by Ryan Moore/The Clarion-Ledger*

Opposite middle: Ole Miss wide receiver Dexter McCluster tries to out maneuver LSU's Chevis Jackson and Curtis Taylor. *Photo by Ryan Moore/The Clarion-Ledger*

Opposite bottom: Ole Miss wide receiver Mike Wallace pulls in a pass as LSU's Chevis Jackson reaches to strip the ball. *Photo by Ryan Moore/The Clarion-Ledger*

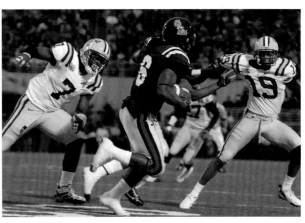

Arkansas

Above: LSU fans cheer on head coach Les Miles and the Tigers as they prepare to face the Arkansas Razorbacks. *Photo by Greg Pearson/The Times*

Left: The LSU Tigers take the field to face the Arkansas Razorbacks at Tiger Stadium in Baton Rouge. *Photo by Greg Pearson/The Times*

Hogs knock Tigers from No. 1 position

By Glenn Guilbeau | Louisiana Gannett News

The college football team formerly known as No. 1 learned the correct pronunciation of Arkansas has nothing to do with Kansas, which now has a much better chance of playing in the national championship game than LSU.

Arkansas destroyed the defense also formerly known as No. 1 and apparently possessed by Lou Tepper with 513 yards of offense, including 206 by tailback Darren McFadden, in a 50-48, triple-overtime victory over the No. 1 Tigers in front of 92,606 at Tiger Stadium.

"Hey, it's A-R-K-A-N-S-A-S," Arkansas offensive guard Robert Felton screamed after the game with the conventional pronunciation of the state, not the "AR-Kansas" pronunciation LSU coach Les Miles used throughout the past week.

"I ain't no AR-Kansas," Felton said. "I bet he knows how to say it now. You can tell him Robert Felton told him. And I'll tell you another thing, anybody who's not behind coach Nutt, you can kiss his tail. That's all I got to say."

Embattled coach Houston Nutt gave Arkansas its first victory over a No. 1 team since it beat Texas in 1981. And Miles can now decide if his future is at LSU or his alma mater Michigan at a less intense pace.

The Tigers (10-2) lost the inside track to the Bowl Championship Series national championship game on Jan. 7 after losing their first November game since 2002, also to Arkansas, and losing at home for the first time in two years. A 13-point underdog, Arkansas improved to 8-4.

"It's devastating to us as a team as a whole and for the coaches and the whole organization and everyone involved in LSU," defensive end Kirston Pittman said.

"This is tough to swallow right now," said tailback Jacob Hester, who led LSU with 126 yards on 28 carries. Hester caught an apparent 54-yard touchdown from Flynn for a 28-21 lead midway in the fourth quarter, but the play was called back because LSU receivers, as they have often done this season, lined up wrong.

"This team's not happy," Miles said. "We understand it cost us. We understand what it means. Nobody's happy. Right now, a goal's off the wall. Zap."

LSU's dream died suddenly at 6:05 p.m. when Arkansas cornerback Matterral Richardson intercepted quarterback Matt Flynn's 2-point-conversion pass to receiver Demetrius Byrd into the end zone, ending the game.

"If they'd have played AR-Kansas, they might have won," Richardson said with a smile.

LSU had just cut Arkansas' lead to 50-48 on a 9-yard touchdown pass from Flynn to receiver Brandon LaFell. Arkansas took a 50-42 lead at the opening of the third overtime on a 3-yard touchdown run by fullback Peyton Hillis and made the mandatory 2-point conversion beginning in overtime period three with a 2-yard run by tailback Felix Jones.

"Ain't going to motivate a team tonight," said Miles, who has to get his crestfallen team up a week from today to play in the Southeastern Conference Championship Game against Georgia or Tennessee in Atlanta. "Tonight, they're going to be sick."

One LSU fan felt that way as he boarded a Tiger Stadium elevator.

"Way too much talent for that (expletive deleted),"

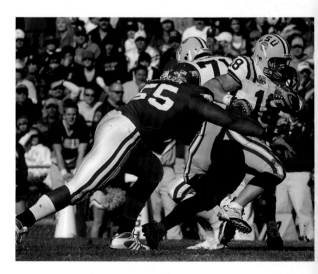

Opposite top: A faithful LSU fan cheers on the Tigers as they take the field to face the Arkansas Razorbacks.
Photo by Greg Pearson/The Times

Opposite bottom: LSU running back Jacob Hester (18) heads downfield with the ball during the first half against Arkansas.
Photo by Greg Pearson/The Times

Left: Arkansas' Darren Mc-Fadden (5) heads downfield with LSU defenders in pursuit.
Photo by Greg Pearson/The Times

he said. "Go to Ann Arbor, Miles."

LSU fans, players and coaches may be replaying in their minds one play over and over. LSU took a 35-28 lead in the first overtime on a 12-yard touchdown run by Flynn and moments later lined up on defense for a fourth-and-10 play by Arkansas from the LSU 25-yard line. Arkansas quarterback Casey Dick dropped back against little rush and calmly found Hillis for a 13-yard gain to the LSU 12. Four plays later, Dick found Hillis again for a 10-yard touchdown and 35-35 tie after the extra point.

LSU never led again and never could stop Arkansas' running game, which totaled 394 yards, including a season-high 328 in regulation. McFadden, who had a 73-yard touchdown run for a 14-6 lead in the third quarter, put Arkansas up 42-35 in the second overtime on a 9-yard touchdown run.

"McFadden's going to play for decades," Miles said. "Certainly, he had a Heisman performance today."

Hester scored on a 2-yard run for a 42-42 tie after the conversion.

The Tigers took a 6-0 lead in the first quarter when they had to settle for field goals twice during great field position. It looked like another classic cardiac LSU finish when Flynn faced a fourth-and-goal in the final minute of regulation and found Byrd for a 2-yard touchdown with 57 seconds to play in the fourth quarter for a 28-28 tie.

Hillis finished with 89 yards rushing and his first three rushing touchdowns of the season on 11 carries and caught five passes for 62 yards and two touchdowns. He gave Arkansas a 21-14 lead in the third quarter on a 65-yard touchdown run up the middle after entering the game with a 14-yard jaunt as his longest run of the season.

"It's a really bad feeling," Pittman said. "We had them on their heels on fourth-and-10. But the quarterback sat back there and found a guy open. It was just a regular, four-man rush, and he had some time to throw the ball. We should've taken advantage of that situation and got off the field."

The 98 points were the most in LSU history and the game took four hours and 20 minutes. LSU lost for the second time this season as the No. 1 team in triple overtime, previously falling 43-37 at Kentucky.

"The national championship's not in reach anymore," Pittman said.

"For three or four hours, all I know is we were the best team in the country today," said Nutt, who improved to 7-1 in overtime games. "We were the best team in the country today." ■

Above: The LSU cheerleaders get the crowd pumped before the Tigers face the Arkansas Razorbacks at Tiger Stadium in Baton Rouge. *Photo by Greg Pearson/The Times*

Opposite left: LSU wide receiver Brandon LaFell (1) has a pass broken up by an Arkansas defender during the first half. *Photo by Greg Pearson/The Times*

Opposite right: LSU defenders take down Arkansas' Darren McFadden during the first half. *Photo by Greg Pearson/The Times*

Arkansas vs. #1 LSU
November 23, 2007 | Baton Rouge, LA

SCORING SUMMARY

Team	1st	2nd	3rd	4th	OT	End
Arkansas	0	7	14	7	22	50
LSU	6	0	15	7	20	48

First quarter
LSU – Colt David 32 field goal 13:19
LSU – David 49 field goal 7:16

Second quarter
UA – Darren McFadden 16 run (Alex Tejada kick) 7:33

Third quarter
UA – McFadden 73 run (Tejada kick) 9:49
LSU – Jacob Hester 12 run (Matt Flynn run) 7:48
UA – Peyton Hillis 65 run (Tejada kick) 1:54
LSU – Demetrius Byrd 7 pass from Flynn (David kick) 2:22

Fourth quarter
UA – Hillis 24 pass from McFadden (Tejada kick) 5:06
LSU – Byrd 2 pass from Flynn (David kick) :57

Overtime
LSU – Flynn 12 run (David kick) 15:00
UA – Hillis 10 pass from Dick (Tejada kick) 15:00
UA – McFadden 9 run (Tejada kick) 15:00
LSU – Hester 2 run (David kick) 15:00
UA – Hillis 3 run (Felix Jones run) 15:00
LSU – Brandon LaFell 9 pass from Flynn (Pass intercepted) 15:00

TEAM STATS

	UA	LSU
First Downs	21	25
Rushes-Yards	53-385	48-204
Passing Yards	128	209
Com-Att-Int	13-24-0	22-47-0
Total Plays	77	95
Total Yards	513	413
Avg. Gain Per Play	6.7	4.3
Fumbles: No.-Lost	3-1	3-0
Penalties: No.-Yards	9-62	4-35
Punt Returns: No.-Yards	3-3	2-11
Kickoff Returns: No.-Yards	6-122	5-104
Interceptions: No.-Yards	0-0	0-0
Possession Time	28:33	31:27
Third-Down Conv.	9-18	11-23
Fourth-Down Conv.	0-1	0-2
Sacks By: No.-Yards	1-7	0-0

INDIVIDUAL STATS: Arkansas

Rushing	No.	Yds	TD	Lg
Darren McFadden	32	206	3	73
Peyton Hillis	11	89	2	65
Felix Jones	9	85	0	31
London Crawford	1	5	0	5

Passing	Att	Com	Int	Yds	TD	Lg
Casey Dick	18	10	0	94	1	16
Darren McFadden	6	3	0	34	1	24

Receiving	No.	Yds	TD	Lg
Peyton Hillis	5	62	2	24
Marcus Monk	2	12	0	7
Felix Jones	2	10	0	5
Lucas Miller	1	16	0	16
D.J. Williams	1	12	0	12
Andrew Davie	1	8	0	8
Robert Johnson	1	8	0	8

Punting	No.	Yds	Avg	Lg
Jeremy Davis	7	255	36.4	53

INDIVIDUAL STATS: LSU

Rushing	No.	Yds	TD	Lg
Jacob Hester	28	126	2	12
Keiland Williams	10	47	0	24
Matt Flynn	9	27	1	12
Charles Scott	1	4	0	4

Passing	Att	Com	Int	Yds	TD	Lg
Matt Flynn	47	22	0	209	3	35

Receiving	No.	Yds	TD	Lg
Early Doucet	7	52	0	12
Demetrius Byrd	6	46	2	12
Richard Dickson	5	69	0	35
Brandon LaFell	3	22	1	10
Charles Scott	1	20	0	20

Punting	No.	Yds	Avg	Lg
Patrick Fisher	8	339	42.4	53

Low on the hog: Underdog Arkansas runs past LSU

By Teddy Allen | The Times

Oops.

Friday afternoon's LSU-Arkansas game rolled on into a chilly late-November evening in Tiger Stadium and carried with it a wave of numbers that a few million poor saps addicted to the game of college football might find interesting.

Here was a game that lasted four-and-a-half hours.

Took three overtimes to settle.

Featured two old rivals playing for a relatively new and unquestionably ugly "Boot" trophy.

Offered for the home team a chance to add to the pair of national championship flags that fly high in the breeze over the east corner of the stadium's north end zone.

Intriguing numbers.

But the big number was that No. 1 BCS ranking LSU padded up to defend against unranked Arkansas. You remember the BCS No. 1 ranking, right? That thing teams this season let go of as if it were a greased pig? — Wait a minute: Friday for LSU, the ranking was just that.

Greased Pigs 50, LSU 48.

"We understand what it's cost us," LSU coach Les Miles said. "We understand what it means."

It means that while LSU will play for the SEC title Saturday in Atlanta, a nice game for sure, winning it no longer assures the Tigers of an invitation to the BCS championship in January an hour down the road in New Orleans. Not after Arkansas did what they did to the Tigers here on the day after Thanksgiving.

Though the Tigers remain undefeated in regulation for the season, they are 10-2 after triple-overtime losses

to both Kentucky and Arkansas. To play for the BCS title, the Tigers need someone to do what they've now done twice: lose.

Miles might have slipped and hit his head on the way to the locker room because he said something strange, even more strange than usual for him, in the moments after the loss. He said the upcoming SEC title game is a "much bigger" game "than the one we just played." Maybe he's lost track of games. Or he's thinking of Michigan's schedule. Regardless, he is not correct — not unless his team's goal was to play in something other than the national championship game. Barring a miracle of BCS proportions, that goal was washed away under Friday's blue sky and in a sea of Arkansas red runners.

"We were the best team in the country today," said Arkansas coach Houston Nutt, whose team is 8-4, 4-4 in the SEC and might have played itself past the PetroSun Independence Bowl.

Arkansas 50, LSU 48. Funny how that happened. The Hogs spent the first quarter perfecting both the fumbled kickoff and the three-plays-and-out routine. But once the Hogs got the hang of it, well, they just about racked up enough yardage to get them back across the state line to Magnolia.

Against an LSU defense that's managed impressive stats but shown unquestionable lapses in things like tackling people and covering opposing receivers, Arkansas rolled to 513 yards, 394 of those on the ground. Running back Darren McFadden, who lined up at quarterback much of the time in Arkansas' "Wild Hog" formation, rushed 32 times for 211 yards. He also threw a touchdown pass. He didn't intercept a pass, but that's just because they didn't let him play defense.

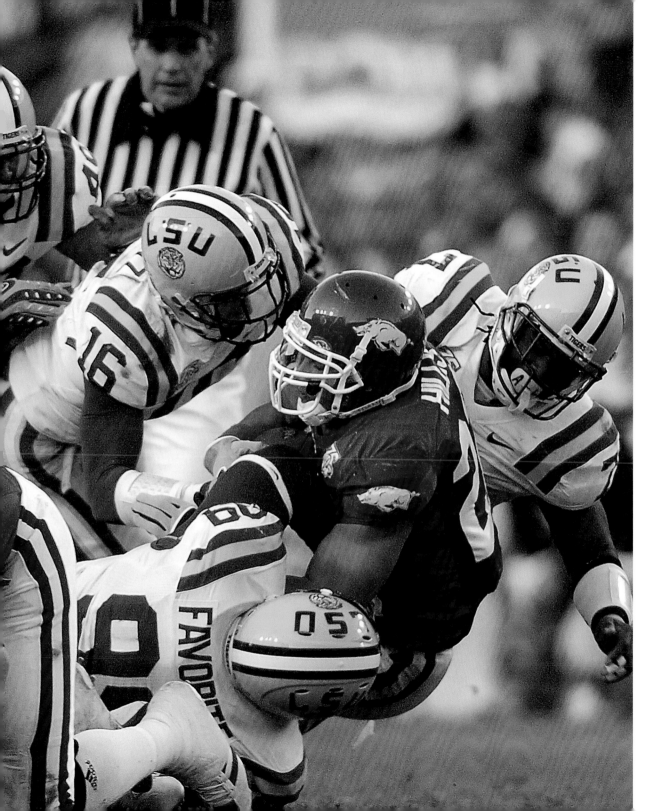

"He deserves the Heisman Trophy," Nutt said, and only a real nut would disagree after this game. "He blocks, catches, quarterbacks, throws, reads; he runs the football with passion and determination…"

Miles put it more simply: "It was hard for us to tackle that guy."

To make matters worse for LSU, McFadden's steady backfield mate, Felix Jones, added 89 yards to his season total of 1,032 coming into the game, and Conway, Ark., senior Peyton Hillis decided to pick this afternoon to challenge McFadden and everyone else in the race for the Heisman. He'd scored three touchdowns and rushed for 238 yards with a long run of 14 yards coming into the LSU game. Friday he had a 65-yard touchdown run, rushed for 89 yards total and scored four touchdowns total, including two in overtime and a key fourth-and-10 reception for a first down in the second overtime when anything less than that would have ended the game with LSU ahead, 35-28.

Whatever Hillis ate yesterday for Thanksgiving, he needs to remember to keep eating that before every game.

Though LSU had trouble getting in gear and trailed 7-6 at halftime, the team was true to its personality by coming back to give the fans their money's worth, either by doing something really good or really bad. The Tigers are nothing if not intriguing. A couple of penalties at inopportune times, a couple of missed tackles, a couple of blown coverages — those things made it interesting, as usual.

For a good part of the second half and even into overtime, it seemed LSU would once again win with another chapter out of its book of Living Right And Rolling The Dice. One Matt Flynn pass intended for Early Doucet was instead caught by Richard Dickson for 35 yards and led to a touchdown. On that same drive on a fourth-and-1, the Tigers ran a lateral, if you can believe

Left: The LSU defense swarms to tackle Arkansas fullback Peyton Hillis. *Photo by Greg Pearson/The Times*

that — and of course converted.

The Tigers tied the game with a minute left to play, but only after lining up to run the fourth-and-goal play, from the 2, three times. One play was halted for an LSU sideline warning, and one apparent LSU touchdown was nullified because the Hogs had called timeout.

LSU scored the next play anyway.

But eventually, the little characteristic miscues and Arkansas' ability to have every answer doomed the Tigers.

And there is that thing called fate. And the law of averages. Maybe those had something to do with the loss as well.

"You can only win so many close games," said Dickson, the Tiger tight end. "It's a mental and physical drag. We've been doing this for so long and it just kind of caught up with us."

A failed LSU 2-point conversion was the final nail that popped the air out of LSU's BCS title balloon. Flynn's pass intended for Demetrius Byrd on a crossing pattern in the back of the north end zone was picked off by Matterral Richardson, who was running wide open when he caught it and didn't stop until he'd reached the jubilant Arkansas sideline, which actually came out to meet him.

Within four minutes, every LSU player, the same ones who'd teamed for a school-record 19-game home winning streak, many of them members of the winningest senior class in school history, all of them who'd been two games away from the national title shot five hours before… every one of those LSU players was gone. No shaking hands, no singing of the alma mater. Just in the tunnel. Off the field.

And gone.

Only Arkansas was still out there. Arkansas was celebrating, as were teams like Kansas and West Virginia and Missouri, teams with a chance to win out and be assured of a title shot. That assurance is something the 2007 live-on-the-edge, die-on-the-edge Tigers no longer likely have. ∎

Opposite: LSU wide receiver Chris Mitchell (86) is sandwiched between two Arkansas defenders as a pass is broken up during the first half.

Photo by Greg Pearson/The Times

Left: LSU wide receiver Demetrius Byrd (2) hauls in a late second half touchdown pass in front of Arkansas' Michael Grant.

Photo by Greg Pearson/The Times

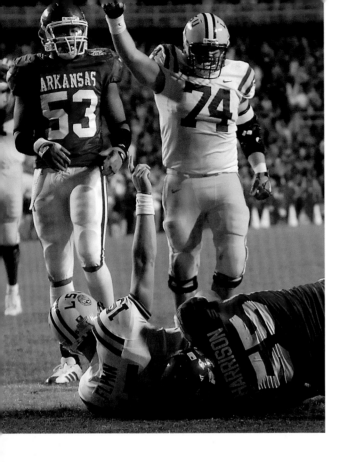

Opposite top left: LSU quarterback Matt Flynn (15) and center Brett Helms (74) celebrate Flynn's late game touchdown against Arkansas. *Photo by Greg Pearson/The Times*

Opposite top right: LSU quarterback Matt Flynn dives into the end zone on a 2-point conversion against Arkansas. *Photo by Greg Pearson/The Times*

Opposite bottom left: LSU running back Jacob Hester (18) fights through tacklers and stretches for a touchdown in the second half against Arkansas. *Photo by Greg Pearson/The Times*

Opposite bottom right: An LSU fan looks for some divine intervention as the Tigers play in overtime against the Arkansas Razorbacks. *Photo by Greg Pearson/The Times*

Left: Arkansas tailback Darren McFadden hurdles LSU defender Craig Steltz during overtime play at Tiger Stadium in Baton Rouge. *Photo by Greg Pearson/The Times*

Below: LSU head coach Les Miles reacts during the second half of his team's triple overtime loss to Arkansas. *Photo by Greg Pearson/The Times*

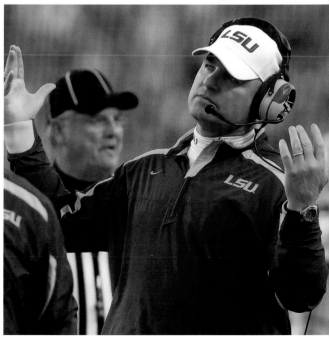

Tennessee

Above: Tennessee tight end Chris Brown (28) crosses the goal line for a Tennessee touchdown during the SEC Championship Game against LSU in the Georgia Dome. *Photo by Sanford Myers/The Tennessean*

Left: LSU coach Les Miles celebrates with his team after winning the SEC Championship Game, 21-14. *Photo by Larry McCormack/The Tennessean*

127

LSU ends see-saw day as conference champs

By Glenn Guilbeau | Louisiana Gannett News

Saturday morning confusion became Saturday night celebration, and it finally looks like LSU has a football coach for years upon years of Saturdays.

"There's no wiggle room," LSU coach Les Miles said, turning down the Michigan job for the umpteenth time following his permanent school's 21-14 victory over Tennessee for the Southeastern Conference championship in the Georgia Dome. "I've got a great place. I'm at home."

With sophomore backup quarterback Ryan Perrilloux throwing for 243 yards and a touchdown to win most valuable player honors and senior cornerback Jonathan Zenon returning an interception 18 yards for the winning touchdown in the fourth quarter, Miles won his first SEC championship. He improved to 33-6 and 11-2 this season with his team headed to the national championship game in his third year as coach, which is apparently just the beginning.

"The sincerity of the relationships between coaches and players — they're real," Miles said and got choked up as he did two weeks ago when Michigan coach Lloyd Carr resigned and Miles' candidacy at his alma mater intensified.

"To think that there's anything less since than the relationship that I have with my team — there's nothing more important," Miles said. "The school here wants me to stay, and this is a great place and I've got a great team. I've got a great recruiting class started, and it would appear that we'd be able to finish it very strongly. There's a lot of plusses right here."

Game day morning did not start out quite so positively, though. An ESPN report said that Miles was

indeed headed to Michigan as head coach.

"I've got a team that's sitting there and they see me," an angry Miles said. "I go down to chapel and when they see me, they're sitting there going, 'Coach, sounds like you're catching a plane on Monday.' That's not true. I had to tell them. I was embarrassed. I was embarrassed that my name was on ESPN. I was embarrassed for my team."

So Miles called his team together to tell them he was remaining its coach and then decided to address the incorrect story at a news conference before the game.

This worked for Perrilloux, who shook off leg and finger injuries to complete 20 of 30 passes with a 27-yard touchdown to receiver Demetrius Byrd for a 13-7 lead early in the third quarter. He also ran in for a 2-point conversion for the 21-14 lead following Zenon's touchdown with 9:54 to play.

"Well, it's definitely good to hear things like that," said Perrilloux, the heir apparent quarterback with injured starter Matt Flynn in his senior year. "We know coach is here with us, and we know coach has been sticking by us from the beginning. And for coach to say that, that definitely put ease on a lot of our people's minds and hearts. We just went out and played for coach, and coach coached for us. And we won as a team —- SEC champs."

Perrilloux started the second game of his career as Flynn was held out because of a shoulder injury suffered in the loss to Arkansas last week.

"We've been trying to get him ready all season," offensive coordinator Gary Crowton said. "We told him early in the week, 'Right now, you're the starter.' Matt could've played if he had to, but Ryan did the job."

Perrilloux completed 14 of 18 passes for 161 yards

Above: Erik Ainge (10) barely gets a pass off under pressure from LSU in the SEC Championship Game.
Photo by Larry McCormack/The Tennessean

Opposite left: Chevis Jackson (21) is too late to stop Chris Brown (28) from scoring UT's first touchdown.
Photo by Larry McCormack/The Tennessean

Opposite top: Arian Foster (27) outruns LSU's Chevis Jackson (21) during the first half. *Photo by Larry McCormack/The Tennessean*

Opposite bottom: Tennessee defensive end Wes Brown (94) assists Tennessee defensive back Nevin McKenzie (20) on a sack of LSU quarterback Ryan Perrilloux (11) during the second quarter.
Photo by Sanford Myers/The Tennessean

Right: Jerod Mayo (7) and Antonio Reynolds (89) stop Jacob Hester (18) from making any more yardage. *Photo by Larry McCormack/The Tennessean*

Opposite: LSU linebacker Darry Beckwith (48) makes the interception in front of Tennessee wide receiver Gerald Jones (4) to stall the Volunteers' drive. *Photo by Sanford Myers/The Tennessean*

in the first half and led the Tigers to a pair of field goal drives in the first quarter, but Tennessee led 7-6 at the half despite a huge statistical advantage by the Tigers of 271 yards to 93.

Tennessee (9-4) took a 7-0 lead on its first possession of the game on an 11-yard touchdown pass from quarterback Erik Ainge to tight end Chris Brown. Perrilloux went to work to start the third quarter, finding receiver Brandon LaFell deep for a 48-yard gain to the UT 21. Then he found Byrd for the 27-yard touchdown and 13-7 lead with 11:52 to play in the period.

UT took a fumble by LSU tailback Trindon Holliday at its 34 and drove 66 yards for a touchdown and a 14-13 lead on a 6-yard touchdown pass from Ainge to receiver Josh Briscoe with 3:09 left in the quarter. Ainge soon fell apart, though, tossing the interception to Zenon in the flat on a third-and-5 from his 14.

"I shouldn't have thrown the ball out there," Ainge said. "I made a bad decision. It's on me."

Ainge drove the Vols to the LSU 14 in the final minutes, but middle linebacker Darry Beckwith intercepted him this time at the LSU 7 and the Tigers ran the clock out for the win. And the celebration began.

"A lot of teams can't call themselves champions, and we can call ourselves champions tonight," Beckwith said.

LSU football secretary Lois Stuckey was hugging everyone in sight.

"After the morning we had, this was wonderful," Stuckey said.

Miles took the large podium at midfield and hoisted the large SEC trophy.

"We never lost a game in regulation this season," Miles said to the roaring purple and gold masses as if he was Huey Long on a stump in Bunkie. "We'll play any team in America."

And Miles wants to be nowhere else in America but in the great state of Louisiana at its flagship school.

"I was worried," assistant coach Bradley Dale Peveto said. "I was worried about learning how to ice fish." ■

Les Miles is an LSU man now

By Bob Heist | The Daily Advertiser

The official media conference had ended, and Les Miles peered to the back of a crowd huddled around him, smiled and raised his right eyebrow.

"There's my wife right there. She's a nice lookin' gal," Miles said. "See her? See her big smile? Yeah."

Seated to Miles' right were his sons, Matthew and Benjamin. In the crowd with his wife Kathy was daughter Kathryn, better known as "Smacker."

A Michigan man? Nah.

Miles addressed that in the harshest terms earlier in the day following a false report from ESPN that he had accepted the head coaching job in Ann Arbor.

Nope, on this Saturday night, Miles was an LSU man. And he's going to remain that way "until the end of his career," according to the school's chancellor, Sean O'Keefe.

Miles is also an SEC champion following a 21-14 win over Tennessee in the Georgia Dome.

It was the end of a day unlike any other in the history of LSU football.

It was the end of a 24-hour period that tugged at the Miles family's heartstrings and fattened their purse.

"This has been the most hectic 24 hours for us. It was so hard to stay focused on this game because so many things took place," Kathy said. "But in the end, it just comes down to we love LSU and Baton Rouge.

"This is where we want to be."

That, however, seemed such an extraordinary stretch with the shadow of Michigan stalking Miles.

It was his alma mater.

He played there and served two stints as an assistant coach with the Wolverines.

It was his dream as a kid in Euclid, Ohio, to play football in the Big House. His dream as a coach was to lead the Blue.

"But you can't be two places at the same time. You can't," Miles said. "When you say no to your alma mater and a team that you love, you're saying a lot about the place that you're at.

"And I'm saying that not just as a football coach — I'm saying that for my family. Easy decision? No. Right decision? You bet. This is home."

And when did an LSU football fan think they'd hear that?

Since Charlie McClendon retired in 1979, Baton Rouge has been looking for an LSU man — a coach that was equal parts successful and comfortable with life in the bayou.

The Tigers went through Jerry Stovall, Bill Arnsparger, Mike Archer, Curley Hallman, Gerry DiNardo and Nick Saban since the end of McClendon's 18 seasons. None stuck more than five years.

Miles, however, has proven different. He's taken LSU to its most prolific three seasons — and wants to stay.

Think about that. Les Miles wants to stay. It was, however, a tough emotional sell.

"I talk to her all the time," Miles said of Kathy sharing in the decision to stay at LSU. "I talk to her at 4 o'clock in the morning, I talk to her at 2 o'clock in the morning ...

"It was (a hard decision); it certainly was. But it's something we're comfortable with."

"I believe this is one of the premier programs in the country; but to pass on Michigan and the Big House? I guess this makes us the Bigger House now," said Board of Supervisors member Stanley Jacobs.

"This (new contract for Miles) was a matter of pride for us. We have the best coach in America — and that sounds a lot better to me than 'had'."

Added SEC title game MVP Ryan Perrilloux, the troubled sophomore quarterback Miles recruited and has slapped on the wrist and suspended more times than any player during his first three years:

"We know coach is here with us, and we know coach has been sticking by us from the beginning. And for coach to say that (he's turning down Michigan), that definitely put ease on a lot of people's minds and hearts.

"We just went out and played for coach."

A coach who said Louisiana was good enough. How's that for a legacy? ∎

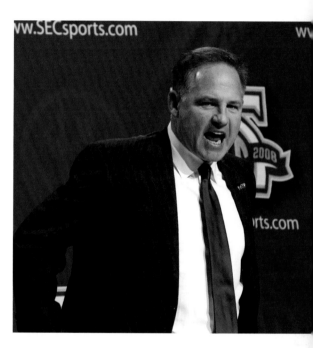

Above: LSU head coach Les Miles refutes ESPN's report that he will leave for the head coaching position at the University of Michigan prior to the SEC Championship Game.
Photo by Larry McCormack/The Tennessean

Opposite: Eric Berry (14) and a host of Tennessee defenders try to stop Keiland Williams during the SEC Championship Game
Photo by Larry McCormack/The Tennessean

#14 Tennessee vs. #7 LSU
December 1, 2007 | Baton Rouge, LA

SCORING SUMMARY

Team	1st	2nd	3rd	4th	End
Tennessee	7	0	7	0	14
LSU	6	0	7	8	21

First quarter
UT – Chris Brown 11 pass from Erik Aigne (Daniel Lincoln kick) 12:00
LSU – Colt David 30 field goal 8:29
LSU – David 30 field goal 3:07
Third quarter
LSU – Demetrius Byrd 27 pass from Ryan Perrilloux (David kick) 11:52
UT – Josh Briscoe 6 pass from Ainge (Lincoln kick) 3:09
Fourth quarter
LSU – Jonathan Zenon 18 interception return (Perrilloux run) 9:54

TEAM STATS

	UT	LSU
First Downs	17	21
Rush-Pass-Penalty	7-10-0	9-12-0
Rushes-Yards	26-94	47-212
Passing Yards	249	252
Com-Att-Int	20-40-2	21-33-1
Total Plays	66	80
Total Yards	343	464
Avg. Gain Per Play	5.2	5.8
Fumbles: No.-Lost	0-0	3-1
Penalties: No.-Yards	0-0	9-44
Punts-Avg.	5-36.0	4-45.0
Punt Returns: No.-Yards	2-11	1-1
Kickoff Returns: No.-Yards	4-99	3-64
Interceptions: No.-Yards	1-15	2-18
Possession Time	23:52	36:08
Third-Down Conv.	4-13	10-20
Fourth-Down Conv.	0-1	1-2
Sacks By: No.-Yards	1-8	0-0

INDIVIDUAL STATS: Tennessee

Rushing	No	Yds	TD	Lg
Arian Foster	21	55	0	11
Gerald Jones	2	39	0	20
Lennon Creer	1	1	0	1
Jonathan Crompton	1	0	0	0

Passing	Att	Com	Int	Yds	TD	Lg
Erik Ainge	40	20	2	249	2	47

INDIVIDUAL STATS: Tennessee

Receiving	No.	Yds	TD	Lg
Josh Briscoe	8	79	1	20
Arian Foster	2	40	0	47
Chris Brown	2	35	1	24
Brad Cottam	2	28	0	19
Lucas Taylor	2	25	0	13
Austin Rogers	2	20	0	15
Denarius Moore	1	16	0	16
Lennon Creer	1	6	0	6

Punting	No.	Yds	Avg	Lg
Britton Colquitt	5	180	36.0	45

INDIVIDUAL STATS: LSU

Rushing	No	Yds	TD	Lg
Jacob Hester	23	120	0	20
Trindon Holliday	6	58	0	19
Keiland Williams	5	34	0	27
Ryan Perrilloux	9	14	0	10
Richard Murphy	1	0	0	0
TEAM	2	-4	0	0
Early Doucet	1	-10	0	0

Passing	Att	Com	Int	Yds	TD	Lg
Ryan Perrilloux	30	20	1	243	1	48
Patrick Fisher	1	1	0	9	0	9

Receiving	No.	Yds	TD	Lg
Early Doucet	5	29	0	23
Demetrius Byrd	4	72	1	27
Brandon LaFell	3	65	0	48
Richard Dickson	2	15	0	8
Richard Murphy	2	14	0	12
Jacob Hester	2	5	0	7
Keith Zinger	1	27	0	27
Charles Scott	1	16	0	16
Quinn Johnson	1	9	0	9

Punting	No.	Yds	Avg	Lg
Patrick Fisher	4	180	45.0	58

Above: Brent Vinson (13) delivers a hit on LSU's Demetrius Byrd to break up a pass in the second half of the SEC Championship Game. *Photo by Larry McCormack/The Tennessean*

Right: Tennessee coach Phillip Fulmer yells for a timeout during the first half of the SEC Championship Game against LSU.
Photo by Larry McCormack/The Tennessean

Far right: LSU running back Trindon Holliday (8) fumbles the ball which Tennessee cornerback Eric Berry (14) would recover during the SEC Championship Game. *Photo by Sanford Myers/The Tennessean*

Above: LSU cornerback Jonathan Zenon (19) makes the interception in front of Tennessee wide receiver Quinton Hancock (87) before returning it for the game-winning touchdown.
Photo by Sanford Myers/The Tennessean

Following left: Tennessee's Quinton Hancock (87) can't catch up with Jonathan Zenon as he returns the interception for LSU's game-winning touchdown in the SEC Championship Game.
Photo by Larry McCormack/The Tennessean

Following right: LSU head coach Les Miles holds up the SEC Championship trophy with his players after defeating UT 21-14 at the Georgia Dome. *Photo by Sanford Myers/The Tennessean*

WESTERN

UNIVERSITY OF ALABAMA
UNIVERSITY OF ARKANSAS
AUBURN UNIVERSITY
LOUISIANA STATE UNIVERSITY
UNIVERSITY OF MISSISSIPPI
MISSISSIPPI STATE UNIVERSITY

EASTERN

UNIVERSITY OF FLORIDA
UNIVERSITY OF GEORGIA
UNIVERSITY OF KENTUCKY
UNIVERSITY OF SOUTH
UNIVERSITY OF TENNESSEE

Ohio State

BCS CHAMPIONSHIP 1.7.08 ■ OHIO STATE **24** | LSU **38**

Above: LSU fans cheer on their team during the BCS championship game. *Photo by Greg Pearson/The Times*

Left: LSU head coach Les Miles points to the heavens after his team defeated the Ohio State Buckeyes in the BCS championship game. *Photo by Greg Pearson/The Times*

LSU makes history with second BCS title

By Glenn Guilbeau | Louisiana Gannett News

Can't See LSU. Can't Catch LSU. Can't Be LSU.

After giving No. 1 Ohio State a 10-0 head start, LSU disappeared from the Buckeyes in the second quarter with three unanswered touchdowns and kept the vanishing act going for a 38-24 victory in the BCS national championship game in front of a Louisiana Superdome record crowd of 79,651.

Most of those were LSU fans. The Tigers (12-2) became the first school to win two national championships in the BCS format, which began in 1998, and the first team since Minnesota in 1960 to win a national championship with two losses. LSU also won the BCS title for the 2003 season on Jan. 4, 2004, in the same Superdome.

"Excuse me ... Wa-Hoo!," LSU coach Les Miles screamed in the postgame news conference after winning his first national championship in his third year with the Tigers. "Just kind of had to do that. Just one of those things."

Miles held the crystal ball high in the celebration ceremony at midfield.

"We enjoy playing in this arena," he said. "We enjoy playing in the state of Louisiana."

Can't Beat LSU here. The Tigers improved to 9-0 in the dome since the 1987 season and 2-0 in national title games.

The "Can't See Me" saying became the players' slogan

this season as they waved hands in front of their faces as if they were invisible after big plays. Well, LSU hands were everywhere throughout most of the night as the Tigers rolled up 326 yards of offense, and Ohio State often seemed to be grasping at air.

In a night to remember, LSU was faster, stronger and craftier as some new offensive plays outfoxed the nation's No. 1-ranked total defense, which came in allowing just 225 yards a game. The Tigers also committed absolutely no penalties in the first half and only four for the game after coming close to leading the nation in that dubious category during the season.

Everyone will now be able to see LSU at the top of the BCS standings and The Associated Press poll as the Tigers won their second BCS national championship in five seasons amid chants of "SEC, SEC, SEC." Florida beat Ohio State last season for the national title. It was

LSU's third national title overall as judged by a major and accepted wire service with the first one coming in 1958.

Fifth-year senior quarterback Matt Flynn threw a career-high four touchdown passes and completed 19 of 27 for 174 yards, and won the most outstanding offensive player award.

"I feel extremely blessed to have this last year and be a part of this great team," said Flynn, who kissed the crystal ball heartily. "We came out here in the right frame of mind and prepared well."

Flynn's 4-yard touchdown pass to wide receiver Early Doucet with 9:04 to play in the third period put the Tigers up 31-10, climaxing an 80-yard drive in 14 plays that started the second half. Flynn hit tight end Richard Dickson for a 5-yard touchdown pass with 1:50 to go for a 38-17 lead.

"We're stubborn," Flynn said. "We knew we'd come

Left: An LSU fan shows his support during the BCS national championship game.
Photo by Greg Pearson/The Times

Middle: LSU fan Eddie Fousch dances to live music outside the Superdome.
Photo by Greg Pearson/The Times

Far left: LSU fans wait, during the Tigers' pep rally in preparation for the BCS championship game in New Orleans.
Photo by Jim Hudelson/The Times

back. We're just stubborn. We don't know when to quit. We don't focus on the things going on around us whether it's good or bad. We've proven that all year. And through the course of the year we became a smarter team."

Dickson caught four passes for 44 yards and two touchdowns. Tailback Jacob Hester led LSU with 86 yards on 21 carries. Tailback Chris Wells led Ohio State with 146 yards on 20 carries and a touchdown.

Ohio State (11-2) apparently stopped LSU's opening drive of the third period when it forced a punt on fourth-and-23 from the LSU 40, but Austin Spitler roughed punter Patrick Fisher for a 15-yard penalty to the Ohio State 45. A third personal foul call against the unraveling Buckeyes gave the Tigers another 15 yards.

Everything appeared to be going LSU's way, but on its next possession Flynn threw a pass toward the sideline without a receiver in the area. Cornerback Malcolm Jenkins intercepted at the LSU 34 and returned it to the Tigers' 11-yard line. On fourth-and-4 from the 5, quarterback Todd Boeckman found wide receiver Brian Robiskie for a touchdown, cutting LSU's lead to 31-17

and disrupting the momentum.

It was only temporary, though. The Buckeyes never got any closer until an academic touchdown with 1:13 to play on a 15-yard pass from Boeckman to receiver Brian Hartline cut LSU's lead to 38-24.

The Tigers came alive with a vengeance and took control of the game in the second quarter, erasing a 10-3 disadvantage and taking a 24-10 halftime lead with three unanswered touchdowns in breathtaking fashion.

After falling behind thanks to a pair of defensive breakdowns, LSU got a field goal in the first quarter and tied it 10-10 on a 13-yard touchdown pass from Flynn to Dickson in the second period. Offensive coordinator Gary Crowton displayed a new formation with four receivers bunched right with Dickson lined up on the left end. The Buckeyes focused on the receiver committee, leaving Dickson open.

"That was a great play," Flynn said. "We just put that in and worked hard on it in the bowl preparation."

Ohio State drove right back down the field in response as Wells ripped off a 29-yard run around left end.

LSU's defense finally toughened and forced a field goal attempt from 38 yards. Defensive tackle Ricky Jean-Francois ended that by knocking offensive guard Ben Pierson into the backfield and stormed in to block it. Middle linebacker Darry Beckwith recovered at the LSU 34. Jean-Francois finished with six tackles and was named the defensive most outstanding player.

"Once I got through and saw the ball, I was like, 'Please let me block the ball,'" Jean-Francois said. "When I finally did, I was just shocked."

After the block, Flynn found receiver Brandon LaFell for a 10-yard touchdown and 17-10 lead with 7:25 to go before halftime.

Backup safety Harry Coleman, subbing for injured starter Craig Steltz, set up the next LSU touchdown. Coleman sprinted in from the secondary just before the snap on a blitz and hurried the pass of Boeckman. Subsequently, Boeckman's deep sideline pass to Ray Small was slightly underthrown and Chevis Jackson intercepted it in stride. Small fell, and Jackson returned his theft 34 yards to the Buckeyes' 24-yard line. That set

Above: LSU's Matt Flynn (15) pitches the ball to Jacob Hester during first-quarter action.
Photo by Mike Silva/The Times

Right: LSU fans had little to cheer about during first-quarter action.
Photo by Mike Silva/The Times

Opposite left: Jim Tressel leads the Buckeyes from the tunnel at the start of the game.
Photo by John Rowland/The Daily Advertiser

Opposite right: Ohio State's Chris Wells (28) breaks free and scores the first touchdown in the BCS national championship game.
Photo by Mike Silva/The Times

up a 1-yard touchdown by Hester for a 24-10 lead with 4:16 to play before halftime.

"That was a quarter we certainly won't make a highlight film of," Ohio State coach Jim Tressel said. "They can beat you in so many ways."

Ohio State took a 7-0 lead on just the fourth play of the game when Wells went up the middle virtually untouched for a 65-yard touchdown just 1:16 into the first quarter, silencing the large LSU contingent in the dome. On Ohio State's next possession, Boeckman found tailback Brandon Saine all alone on the sideline for a 44-yard gain to the LSU 15. That set up a 25-yard field goal by Ryan Pretorius for a 10-0 Ohio State lead with 9:12 to play in the first quarter. The Buckeyes already had 128 yards on two possessions.

LSU recovered with an impressive 65-yard drive of its own in 14 plays, but it stalled and Colt David hit a 32-yard field goal to cut the lead to 10-3 with 2:21 to play in the first period. Down 10-0, Miles basically said, "What, me worry?"

"There's no panic in this team," he said. "Are you kidding me?"

Miles hugged Jean-Francois hard on the way off the field.

"I'm 2-0, coach," said Jean-Francois, who missed the whole regular season because of an academic suspension before playing in two games — the SEC Championship Game and the national championship.

"He's got the right stuff," Miles said.

"I just feel like I'm on the top of the world," Jean-Francois said.

He was not alone. ∎

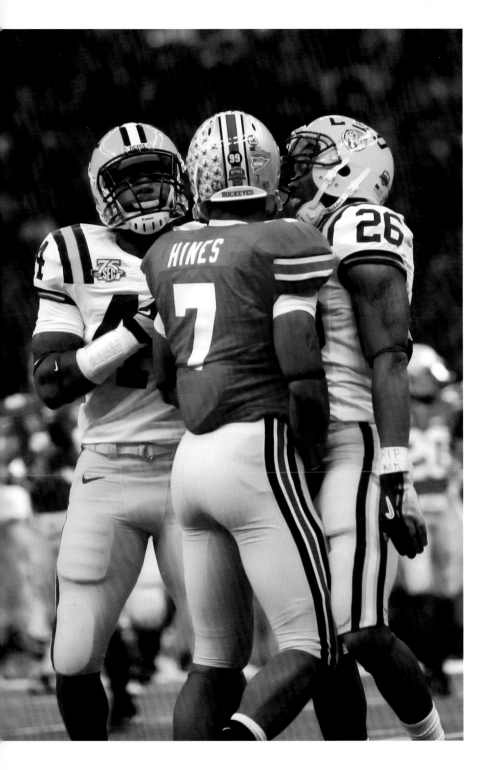

Above: LSU's Chad Jones fumbles the ball in first-quarter action. LSU recovered the fumble. *Photo by Mike Silva/The Times*

Left: LSU's Danny McCray (44) and Richard Murphy (26) get in the face of Ohio State's Jermale Hines' face in first-quarter action. *Photo by Mike Silva/The Times*

Opposite: LSU's Matt Flynn is brought down by Ohio State's Cameron Heyward and Larry Grant. *Photo by John Rowland/The Daily Advertiser*

Comeback Kids walk away with the trophy

By Bob Heist | The Daily Advertiser

As coach Les Miles hoisted the latest addition to LSU's crystal collection through a cloud of purple and yellow confetti, the most amazing journey in college football this season had ended.

But every ending — this one as the Bowl Championship Series national champion following LSU's 38-24 win over Ohio State in the Superdome — has a beginning. And as far as the Tigers are concerned, this wacky season actually provided seven.

An explanation is in order.

These national champions — the school's third and the fourth in the BCS era for the Southeastern Conference — were just plays away from 12-2 becoming 8-4. And, honestly, maybe worse.

Tiptoeing through a schedule filled with speed traps (they don't have those in the Big Ten, just potholes) the Tigers trailed seven times during the season. And that included the 10-0 jump-start Ohio State grabbed less than six minutes into the title game.

Let's relive the Comeback Kids' experience.

• Sept. 22: LSU fell behind No. 12 South Carolina 7-0, then reeled off the next 28 points. Tigers win 28-16.

• Sept. 29: Undermanned Tulane grabs a 9-7 lead. LSU closes with the game's final 27 points. Tigers win 34-9.

• Oct. 6: No. 9 Florida three times leads by double

Left: LSU's Colt David (6) and holder/QB Matt Flynn (15) celebrate after an extra point to tie the game in the first quarter.
Photo by Jim Hudelson/The Times

Below: Ohio State wide receiver Brian Robiskie (left) loses the football in the end zone after having a pass broken up by LSU's Chevis Jackson in the first half.
Photo by Greg Pearson/The Times

Far left: LSU's Richard Dickson (82) runs in for a TD in the first quarter.
Photo by Jim Hudelson/The Times

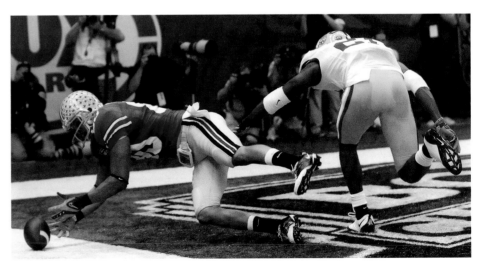

digits, the last at 24-14. LSU strikes for two touchdowns in the final 10:05 and a 28-24 win.

• Oct. 20: No. 18 Auburn builds a 17-7 lead by halftime. LSU then scores 23 of the game's final 30 points, including the game-winning pass from Matt Flynn to Demetrius Byrd with one second on the clock — Tigers 30-24.

• Nov. 3: In the Saban Bowl, LSU rallies to score two touchdowns in the final 2:49 of the game for a 41-34 win over No. 17 Alabama.

• Dec. 1: For the SEC championship, No. 14 Tennessee scores a touchdown on its opening possession. Later trailing by a point, LSU rallies for a 21-14 win on Jonathan Zenon's interception return for a score in the fourth quarter.

All the talk over the last week hinged on speed vs. brawn. On how a year after having its skirt hiked and its flaws revealed by Florida, proud Ohio State was going to set the record straight on that 0-8 record in bowl games against the SEC.

Maybe what should have been addressed was character, since that would appear to be a characteristic consistent with a champion.

"This team is tough. Just tough," said quarterback Matt Flynn, named the game's Offensive MVP after passing for a career-high four touchdowns. "We just don't quit — no matter the score, no matter the eventual outcome. We did that all season and it got us here. We did it again tonight and won a national championship because of it."

So what we're left with is a dynasty. And don't question that.

LSU is the first program (sorry, USC) to win two BCS championships, and the best in BCS bowl games with four wins in four tries.

All that from a two-loss, this-close-to-four-or-more team that needed several miracles to remain a dog in the title hunt, and then two more the night of Dec. 1 for a shot at the national championship.

And then they're down 10 points to Ohio State — and win by 14.

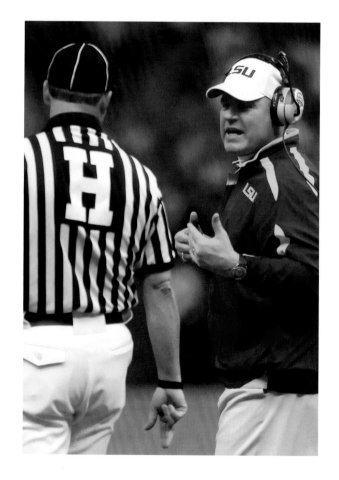

Above: LSU's Darry Beckwith celebrates after LSU blocked an Ohio State field goal attempt. *Photo by John Rowland/The Daily Advertiser*

Left: LSU head coach Les Miles talks with an official. *Photo by Greg Pearson/The Times*

Top left: Ohio State's Brian Robiskie picks up yardage after a catch. *Photo by John Rowland/The Daily Advertiser*

The SEC is king, again. The crown for the next year will reside in Baton Rouge.

"Football's a tough, physical game (in the SEC), week in and week out," conference commissioner Mike Slive said. "Look at LSU. They're down 10 points, but they've been in that situation before. It happens (in the SEC) because of the competitive nature of our teams.

"Does it prove anything? It proves that the best team — again — is from our conference. Any conclusions that need to be drawn, I think, can be done from that." ■

Above: LSU wide receiver Trindon Holliday (8) tries to elude an Ohio State defensive player after making a catch.
Photo by Greg Pearson/The Times

#2 LSU vs. #1 Ohio State
January 7, 2008 | New Orleans, LA

SCORING SUMMARY

Team	1st	2nd	3rd	4th	End
LSU	3	21	7	7	38
Ohio State	10	0	7	7	24

First Quarter
OSU – Chris Wells 65 run (Ryan Pretorius kick), 13:34
OSU – Pretorius 25 field goal, 9:12
LSU – Colt David 32 field goal, 2:21

Second Quarter
LSU – Richard Dickson 13 pass from Matt Flynn (David kick), 13:00
LSU – Brandon LaFell 10 pass from Flynn (David kick), 7:25
LSU – Jacob Hester 1 run (David kick), 4:16

Third Quarter
LSU – Early Doucet 4 pass from Flynn (David kick), 5:56
OSU – Brian Robiskie 5 pass from Todd Boeckman (Pretorius kick) 1:38

Fourth Quarter
LSU – Dickson 5 pass from Flynn (David kick), 1:50
OSU – Brian Hartline 15 pass from Boeckman (Pretorious kick), 1:13

TEAM STATS

	LSU	OSU
First Downs	25	17
Rush-Pass-Penalty	12-9-4	6-10-1
Rushes-Yards	49-152	30-145
Passing Yards	174	208
Com-Att-Int	19-27-1	15-26-2
Total Plays	76	56
Total Yards	326	353
Avg. Gain Per Play	4.3	6.3
Fumbles: No.-Lost	2-0	3-1
Penalties: No.-Yards	4-36	7-83
Punts-Avg.	3-56.7	3-50.0
Punt Returns: No.-Yards	1-8	1-9
Kickoff Returns: No.-Yards	2-22	7-17.7
Interceptions: No.-Yards	2-38	1-23
Possession Time	33:56	26:04
Third-Down Conv.	11-18	3-13
Fourth-Down Conv.	1-1	2-3
Sacks By: No.-Yards	5-36	1-15

INDIVIDUAL STATS: LSU

Rushing	No.	Yds.	TD	Lg
Jacob Hester	21	86	1	20
Richard Murphy	2	33	0	24
Keiland Williams	2	20	0	20
Trindon Holliday	3	13	0	9
Matt Flynn	12	8	0	9
Early Doucet	2	7	0	4
Charles Scott	2	6	0	5
Ryan Perrilloux	1	4	0	4
TEAM	4	-25	0	0

Passing	Att	Com	Int	Yds	TD	Lg
Matt Flynn	27	19	1	174	4	20

Receiving	No.	Yds.	TD	Lg
Early Doucet	7	51	1	16
Richard Dickson	4	44	2	15
Demetrius Byrd	2	28	0	20
Brandon LaFell	2	15	1	10
Keith Zinger	1	18	0	18
Charles Scott	1	16	0	16
Quinn Johnson	1	3	0	3
Keiland Williams	1	-1	0	0

Punting	No.	Yds	Avg	Lg
Patrick Fisher	3	170	56.7	62

INDIVIDUAL STATS: Ohio State

Rushing	No.	Yds	TD	Lg
Chris Wells	20	146	1	65
Brian Hartline	1	6	0	6
Todd Boeckman	9	-7	0	21

Passing	Att	Com	Int	Yds	TD	Lg
Todd Boeckman	26	15	2	208	2	44

Receiving	No.	Yds	TD	Lg
Brian Hartline	6	75	1	17
Brian Robiskie	5	50	1	19
Brandon Saine	3	69	0	44
Ray Small	1	14	0	14

Punting	No.	Yds	Avg.	Lg
A.J. Trapasso	3	150	50.0	63

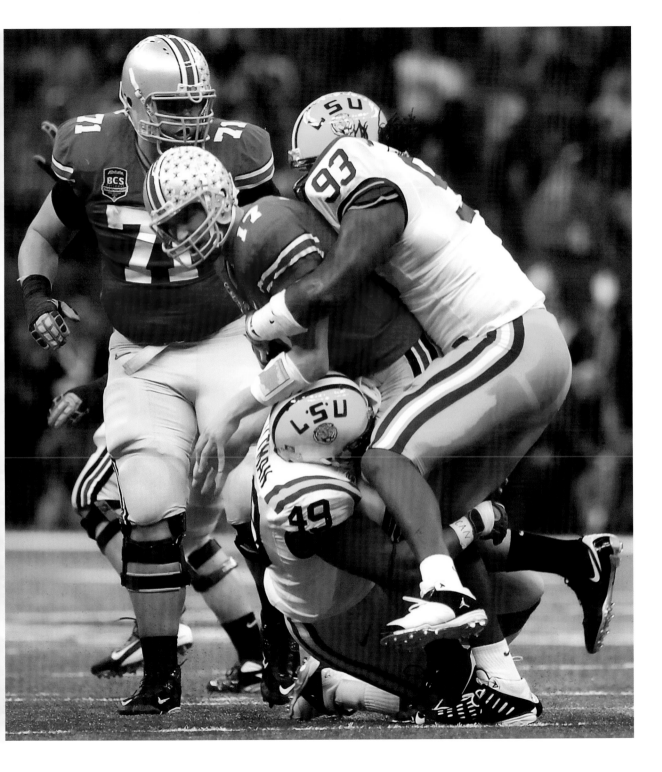

Above: LSU tight end Richard Dickson celebrates a first-half touchdown against Ohio State. *Photo by Greg Pearson/The Times*

Left: LSU players Tyson Jackson (93) and Kirston Pittman (49) wrap up Ohio State quarterback Todd Boeckman for a sack. *Photo by Greg Pearson/The Times*

Opposite: LSU tight end Keith Zinger (89) makes a play as Ohio State's Malcolm Jenkins attempts to make a tackle. *Photo by Greg Pearson/The Times*

LSU clearly best team in the land

By Bob Tompkins | The Town Talk

Outlined against a black and blue Big Ten team, the Southeastern Conference rose again.

Last year, the SEC team was Florida. This year, LSU. Both times, the Big Ten team to play the SEC team's foil was Ohio State.

At stake was the BCS championship. OSU got off to a quick start both times, only to falter to a more talented and, yes, speedy team.

All hail the new champion, LSU, a 38-24 victor over the top-ranked Buckeyes. It took 45 years between the last two national football titles for LSU. This time it took just four, making the 12-2 Tigers the first team to win two BCS national championships and the first two-loss team to do so.

Was OSU overrated, or was LSU that much better?

Keep in mind, Ohio State's defense had allowed just two rushing touchdowns all season. Two rushing touchdowns all season. That's not something to sniff at. It's downright impressive.

Yet, the OSU defense wasn't up to the challenge of defending LSU.

Left: LSU's Early Doucet (9) is congratulated by Jacob Hester (18) after Doucet's third-quarter touchdown. *Photo by Jim Hudelson/The Times*

Opposite: LSU defensive back Chevis Jackson (21) heads downfield with the ball after making an interception during the first half. *Photo by Greg Pearson/The Times*

Here's what I think: A great Ohio State defense couldn't stop LSU's offense, and a decent Ohio State offense couldn't take advantage of LSU's defense, even though its All-American strong safety didn't play more than half of the game.

Here are a couple of things to remember about this game. With the score tied 10-10, LSU blocked a field goal. With LSU leading just 17-10 and facing a third-and-goal at the 1 late in the second quarter, Jacob Hester followed his offensive line just far enough to put the ball over the goal line for an eventual 24-10 lead.

OSU, unaccustomed to giving up rushing touchdowns, looked as if it might put together a goal-line stand or at least hold LSU to a field goal. But it didn't, and it gave the Tigers a huge advantage going to the locker room at halftime.

The defensive play that set up that touchdown drive may have been equally as telling.

With senior All-American strong safety Craig Steltz sidelined with a shoulder stinger, his replacement, sophomore Harry Coleman blitzed on a third down, and cornerback Chevis Jackson made a one-handed interception of a Todd Boeckman pass and returned it 34 yards.

This is reflective of how LSU in this game, as well as it did through the season, didn't skip a beat when a star went down.

Quarterback Matt Flynn, other than one interception, was as efficient as any coach could ask of a quarterback and was deserving of the game's Offensive MVP award for his cool leadership, his sharp passing and, maybe best of all, his ability to read the defensive schemes of an OSU defense that does an excellent job of disguising its defenses.

Ricky Jean-Francois, a sophomore defensive tackle who got his first action of the season in the SEC title game because of a suspension for an off-the-field issue,

was the game's Defensive MVP, and a deserving choice, making a ton of tackles and blocking a 38-yard field goal when the score was tied 10-10.

That helped break any chance the Buckeyes had of changing the momentum.

Ultimately, though, there were a galaxy of stars on offense and defense for the Tigers. Ultimately, this was an LSU team that realized its potential at the best possible time.

And LSU coach Les Miles became the first coach in a single season to beat five coaches who won a national championship: Steve Spurrier, Urban Meyer, Nick Saban, Phil Fulmer and Tressel.

It's time for LSU fans to celebrate it all. And for those who wanted to push for Southern Cal or Georgia or any other team as a team that really should have won it all, the answer is: Afraid not.

LSU is clearly the best college team in the land. ∎

Above: LSU's Matt Flynn throws a pass during the BCS championship game. *Photo by John Rowland/The Daily Advertiser*

Left: The LSU defense gets to Ohio State's QB Todd Boeckman (17) during the third quarter. *Photo by Jim Hudelson/The Times*

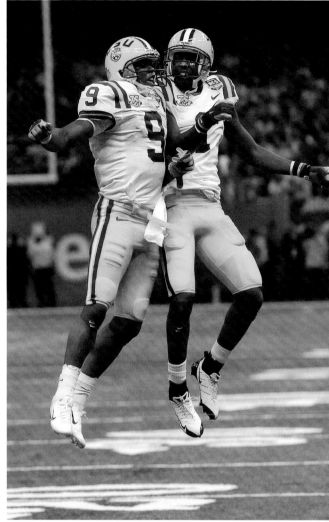

Above: LSU wide receivers Early Doucet (9) and Brandon LaFell celebrate Doucet's second-half touchdown.
Photo by Greg Pearson/The Times

Left: LSU's Matt Flynn is taken down by Ohio State's Marcus Freeman and Malcolm Jenkins. *Photo by John Rowland/The Daily Advertiser*

Miles proves he's his own man, his own hero

By Roy Lang III | The Times

Nick, shmick.

Try telling LSU folks Les Miles is winning with Nick Saban's players now. Sure, it's partially true – some of Saban's recruits helped the Tigers to another national championship – but Nick wasn't here to "coach" them through one of the most trying college football seasons to date.

LSU's 38-24 victory over the Ohio State Buckeyes in the Allstate BCS National Championship Game at the Louisiana Superdome encapsulated a bizarre 2007 campaign and proved the mettle of the players in purple and gold and the man dubbed "The Hat."

"Being down 10 wasn't going to bother us," Miles said. "We've been down 10 before."

Multiple times this season.

"I'm glad this is over," LSU quarterback Matt Flynn said. "It just feels incredible. I'm just so blessed to be part of such a great team, great guys, and it's so sweet to end it this way."

Call Miles a gambler, call him a kook, call him flighty; just don't forget to call him beloved – soon to be more than his predecessor.

Miles got his team focused. The Tigers weren't the squad to implode due to penalties. They watched Ohio State do that this time.

Above: Ohio State's Brian Robiskie catches a touchdown pass in the third quarter. *Photo by John Rowland/The Daily Advertiser*

Left: LSU's Ciron Black (70) has a fan in the stands. *Photo by Mike Silva/The Times.*

Far left: LSU coach Les Miles stands with his team on the field before the BCS championship game. *Photo by Jim Hudelson/The Times*

Miles helped a team through injuries, a pair of triple-overtime losses and several equally emotional evenings in victory.

Miles made an impassioned plea to his team, just prior to the SEC Championship Game. He made sure they knew he was staying. What ensued wasn't the best game of the season, but it was a win – one that punched the ticket to New Orleans and made a national title a possibility.

Saban made no such pleas here. He didn't have to -- it's a free country, but there's something to be said for not constantly heading for the seemingly greener grass.

Now, Baton Rouge and the rest of Tiger Nation won't be able to deny Miles' ability. He will, as Saban did, breed love and support.

In fact, Miles may become even more popular and heroic.

He could have gone to Michigan. The Wolverines would have opened the Brink's trucks. Instead, he decided to stay in the South for his chance to beat those hated Buckeyes.

He's a better people person and a pretty good coach.

Fans will appreciate his dedication, his long-term commitment to the Tigers and, of course, the Ws. Miles' attitude is more fan-friendly. To fans of Tiger Nation, he looks like one of them. He wears a ball cap and his emotions on his sleeve.

In the ensuing moments after the win, BCS officials handed Miles a leather jacket to wear during the coronation ceremony. He shunned the gesture to wear the black jacket, instead wanting to proudly display his purple and gold colors.

"I'm LSU," Miles said repeatedly. He caved eventually, but it's not hard to see where his heart lies.

Don't forget the appeal of his wild-card persona. He says he doesn't like the moniker, as it makes him appear irresponsible. He should embrace it, fans will.

Miles used one more fourth-down gamble to cement LSU's victory when Matt Flynn found just enough real estate on a keeper to keep the chains and the clock moving late in the fourth quarter.

In three years, Miles' success has been incredible. He

Left: LSU's Ricky Jean-Francois (90) celebrates in the fourth quarter.

Photo by Jim Hudelson/The Times

Far left: LSU's Harry Coleman (24) celebrates after his fourth-quarter fumble recovery.

Photo by Jim Hudelson/The Times

has a national title, three seasons of at least 11 wins, a 34-6 record and three dominating victories in three bowl games.

"This is a very special season and a very special team," Miles said. "To enjoy the position we're in at LSU, standing atop college football, I'm very emotional."

He's different, for sure. Even in victory, he proved that. Miles opened his postgame news conference with a comment or two before pausing and then screaming … "Yaaaaaahhhooooooooo!"

Fans and members of the media – this journalist included – are often left shaking their heads at Miles.

Now, the only appropriate action is to tip our caps. ∎

Top: LSU's Curtis Taylor comes up with an interception to kill an Ohio State drive. *Photo by John Rowland/The Daily Advertiser*

Bottom left: LSU's Early Doucet jumps over Ohio State's James Laurinaitis. *Photo by John Rowland/The Daily Advertiser*

Bottom right: LSU running back Jacob Hester (18) moves through traffic. *Photo by Greg Pearson/The Times*

Opposite: LSU's Richard Murphy (26) jumps over Ohio State's Anderson Russell (21) in the fourth quarter.
Photo by Jim Hudelson/The Times

Above: LSU quarterback Matt Flynn (15) looks downfield for an open receiver in the second half.
Photo by Greg Pearson/The Times

Right: LSU defensive tackle Glenn Dorsey gets the crowd involved in the second half.
Photo by Greg Pearson/The Times

Opposite: The football flies out of Ohio State quarterback Todd Boeckman's (17) hands as he is hit by LSU defenders Ricky Jean-Francois (90) and Ali Highsmith (7). *Photo by Greg Pearson/The Times*

Left: The Buckeye bench is somber as the last seconds of the game tick off. *Photo by John Rowland/The Daily Advertiser*

Opposite: LSU's Richard Dickson catches a touchdown pass for LSU's final touchdown during the BCS championship game. *Photo by John Rowland/The Daily Advertiser*

Left: Fans celebrate in the fourth quarter.
Photo by Mike Silva/The Times

Opposite: Coach Les Miles and the team celebrate in the final seconds of the BCS championship game.
Photo by Jim Hudelson/The Times

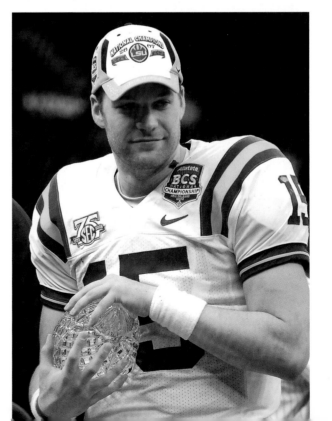

Above: Celebrating LSU's victory in the BCS national championship game.
Photo by Mike Silva/The Times

Left: LSU quarterback Matt Flynn cradles the Coaches' Trophy after his team defeated the Ohio State Buckeyes in the BCS national championship game.
Photo by Greg Pearson/The Times

Far left: Coach Les Miles and his team celebrate the BCS national championship.
Photo by Jim Hudelson/The Times

Above: LSU's Ricky Jean-Francois holds the Coaches' Trophy. *Photo by John Rowland/The Daily Advertiser*

Left: LSU head coach Les Miles holds up the Coaches' Trophy after defeating the Ohio State Buckeyes in the BCS national championship game. *Photo by Greg Pearson/The Times*

Above: Drake Nevis tries to find someone in the crowd with the help of a cell phone. *Photo by John Rowland/The Daily Advertiser*

Top right: LSU's Glenn Dorsey (72) hugs a family member after the win in the BCS national championship game. *Photo by Jim Hudelson/The Times*

Bottom right: LSU coach Les Miles celebrates his victory. *Photo by Mike Silva/The Times*

Above: LSU coach Les Miles and the team sing the school's alma mater. *Photo by John Rowland/The Daily Advertiser*

Following: LSU defensive end Ricky Jean-Francois kisses the Coaches' Trophy after winning the BCS national championship game. *Photo by Greg Pearson/The Times*

Right: The LSU team celebrates as they prepare for interviews with the FOX television crew after defeating the Ohio State Buckeyes 38-24 in the BCS national championship game.
Photo by Greg Pearson/The Times

Far right: LSU coach Les Miles leaves the field of the Superdome after winning the national championship. *Photo by John Rowland/The Daily Advertiser*

Below: LSU wide receiver Brandon LaFell celebrates his team's victory after the BCS national championship game.
Photo by Greg Pearson/The Times

THE DAILY ADVERTISER

Tuesday, January 8, 2008
theadvertiser.com
50 cents ★

38 LSU — BCS CHAMPIONSHIP — 24 Ohio State

TAKE TWO!

LSU makes history with 2nd BCS title

LSU coach Les Miles, left, and his football team point to the fans after defeating Ohio State, 38-24, to claim the BCS Championship at the Superdome in New Orleans on Monday.
The Associated Press

Bruce Brown
bbrown@theadvertiser.com

In the end, history came easily.

LSU's Fightin' Tigers spotted Ohio State a 10-0 advantage, then roared back for a dominating 38-24 victory on Monday in the BCS Championship before 79,651 people in the Louisiana Superdome.

It was the Bayou State's own backyard barbecue, as the Tigers became the first team to capture two BCS Championship trophies as well as the first such champion with two losses.

LSU also won its second BCS Championship in four years while coach Les Miles became the first coach to defeat five coaches in one season who won a national championship: Steve Spurrier, Phillip Fulmer, Urban Meyer, Nick Saban and OSU's Jim Tressel.

And, unlike the 2003 campaign, when LSU defeated Oklahoma in the Superdome to earn the BCS crown and Southern California was named champion by the Associated Press, this time the title is sure to be an undisputed one.

Senior quarterback Matt Flynn led the victory march, throwing for a career-high four touchdowns to earn Most Outstanding Player honors on the night. Ohio State got a 65-yard Chris Wells touchdown

See LSU on Page 7A

Complete coverage from the Superdome

- Comeback kids: Relive LSU's wacky season, **1D**
- Undisputed: Tigers are clearly No. 1, **3D**
- Faster, stronger, craftier LSU outlasts OSU, **3D**
- Offensive Player of the Game: Matt Flynn, **4D**
- Interception changes game's momentum, **4D**
- Facts and stats: The game by the numbers, **5D**
- More photos from the championship win, **6D**

Find bonus coverage @ theadvertiser.com

Council lineup heralds change

Many have high expectations for new members

Amanda McElfresh
amcelfresh@theadvertiser.com

One of the most drastic changes in Lafayette leadership took place Monday as eight new members of the city-parish council were sworn into office.

Only Bruce Conque will return as a member of the council. Conque is entering his second term in office.

"This is an extremely historic day," said City-Parish President Joey Durel, who also took his oath of office for his second term. "You've not seen such a sweeping change in leadership in this community. It's a generational change, and expectations are high."

Durel encouraged the council to remember the principles of working together and having a long-term vision for the community.

"We're all on the same team," Durel said. "I encourage

See COUNCIL on Page 8A

Want to go?
The first 2008 meeting of the Lafayette City-Parish Council will be at 5:30 p.m. today at City Hall, 705 W. University Ave.

Nine men indicted on drug charges

7 in group from area; allegedly tied to L.A. gang

Amanda McElfresh
amcelfresh@theadvertiser.com

A federal grand jury has indicted nine men on various federal charges following an investigation into gang activity.

Seven of the men are from the Acadiana area. One is from Los Angeles, and another is from Texas.

A two-year investigation by the Federal Bureau of Investigation indicated that members of the Cuatro Flats gang, based in Los Angeles, were transporting drugs and stolen vehicles to Louisiana to distribute to local gangs.

The nine men were initially indicted on the federal charges Oct. 11, but the indictment was made public Monday. U.S. Attorney Donald Washington said indictments may remain sealed until an investigation is complete.

See CHARGES on Page 6A

A NOTE TO OUR READERS
We extended our deadlines last night so we could provide complete coverage of the BCS National Championship game. Because of this, some newspapers might be delivered later than usual today.

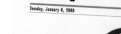

38 LSU — BCS — 24 Ohio State

PURPLE REIGN

Tigers first program to win two BCS championships

LSU quarterback Matt Flynn kisses the national championship crystal trophy as purple and gold confetti falls around him after the LSU Tigers defeated the Ohio State Buckeyes in the BCS Championship game at the Superdome in New Orleans.

THE STAR
Matt Flynn's four touchdown passes baffle Ohio State's No. 1 ranked defense.
Story • 4D

THE GAME
'Can't See Me' Tigers prove too much for the Ohio State Buckeyes.
Story • 3D

THE DEFENSE

SPECIAL SECTION ON MONDAY NIGHT'S BCS TITLE GAME • PA

VICTORIOUS AGAIN

Tigers humble Ohio State in BCS title game

...stronger, ...y face losses, ...nty remains

1958 2003 2007
NATIONAL CHAMPIONS
www.thetowntalk.com
The Town Talk   Tuesday, January 8, 2008

LSU — BCS NATIONAL CHAMPIONSHIP — OHIO STATE

ON TOP TO STAY

Tigers turn back Buckeyes for LSU's third national title

By Glenn Guilbeau
Gannett Louisiana News

38
24

THE TOWN TALK

A4: HEARING ON JENA RALLY POSTPONED | **B1:** RAPIDES' WEST WEIGHING OPTIONS

THE TOWN TALK

www.thetowntalk.com

Tuesday, January 8, 2008 | Alexandria-Pineville, Louisiana | ★ 50¢

BCS CHAMPIONSHIP | LSU 38, OHIO STATE 24

BCSEQUEL FOR LSU

Tigers claim second title in 4 seasons behind strong 2nd quarter

COVERAGE INSIDE

SPECIAL 8-PAGE SECTION

C2 Bob Tompkins says the SEC dominated the Big Ten for the second straight season

C2 LSU quarterback Matt Flynn was the named the game's Offensive Most Valuable Player

C2 Chevis Jackson's second-quarter interception proved to be a turning point

C2 Louisiana College football coach Dennis Dunn offers his grades on how LSU and Ohio State performed

C3 Quarter-by-quarter drive charts from the game

C4 Gannett Louisiana's Bob Heist says a comeback Monday was only fitting for LSU

C5 Gannett Louisiana's Teddy Allen says LSU's victory was picture perfect

C6 Scenes from inside the Louisiana Superdome

C7 Tickets to Monday's game proved to be not only costly, but hard to come by

C8 A look back at LSU's championship season

OTHER COVERAGE

A3 Area LSU fans didn't need to have tickets to have a good time watching the Tigers

A3 Not everyone in Central Louisiana was caught up in Tiger fever

A3 One pupil stood out at Peabody Montessori Monday amidst a sea of purple and gold

ON THE WEB

For more coverage of the BCS Championship game, go to www.thetowntalk.com, and look for the LSU Central link. There, you'll find more stories and photo galleries.

LSU quarterback Matt Flynn (15) celebrates after throwing one of his four touchdown passes in the Tigers' 38-24 victory over Ohio State in the Louisiana Superdome as LSU won its second BCS Championship in four seasons.

INSIDE
Advice........E2 Classified.......D3 Opinions.....B4
Amusement...E4 Comics........E4 Sports.........B1
Area............A4 Living..........E1 US&World...D1
Business.......B6 Cents..........A3

Subscriber Services
1-800-292-0581
Classified Advertising
(318) 487-6363

WEATHER
80% chance of rain
High: 74
Low: 50

01/8/2008 1C

CYAN PLATE MAGENTA PLATE YELLOW PLATE BLACK PLATE

The Times
BCS NATIONAL CHAMPIONSHIP
*TUESDAY, JANUARY 8, 2008

38 **24**

Tiger two-step
LSU claims second national title of BCS era

ROY LANG III
OPINION
rlang@gannett.com

LSU maintains Superdome superiority
By Glenn Guilbeau
gguilbeau@gannett.com

LSU coach Les Miles holds up the BCS national championship trophy after the Tigers defeated Ohio State on Monday night in New Orleans.
Greg Pearson/The Times

Miles proves he's his own man, own hero

NEW ORLEANS — Nick, shmick. Try telling LSU folks Les Miles is winning with Nick Saban's players now. Sure, it's partially true — some of Saban's recruits helped the Tigers to another national championship Monday day — but Nick wasn't here to "coach" them through one of the most trying college football seasons to date.

LSU's 38-24 victory over the Ohio State Buckeyes in the Allstate BCS National Championship Game at the Louisiana Superdome encapsulated a bizarre 2007 campaign and proved the mettle of the players in purple and gold and the man dubbed "The Hat."

"Being down 10 wasn't going to bother us," Miles said. "We've been down 10 before."

Multiple times this season.

"I'm glad this is over," LSU quarterback Matt Flynn said. "It just feels incredible. I'm just so blessed to be part of such a great team, great guys, and it's so sweet to end it this way."

Call Miles a gambler, call him a kook, call him flighty; just don't forget to call him beloved — soon to be more than his predecessor.

Miles got his team focused. The Tigers weren't the squad to implode due to penalties. They watched Ohio State do that this time.

Miles helped a team through injuries, a pair of triple-overtime losses and several equally emotional evenings in victory.

Miles made an impassioned plea to his team just prior to the SEC Championship. He made sure they knew he was staying. What ensued wasn't the best game of the season, but it was a win — one that punched the ticket to Monday night's affair and made a national title a possibility.

Saban made no such pleas here. He didn't have to — it's a new country, but there's something to be said for not constantly heading for the seemingly greener grass.

Now, Baton Rouge and the rest of Tiger Nation won't be able to deny Miles' ability. He will, as Saban did, breed love and support.

In fact, Miles may become even more popular and heroic.

He could have gone to Michigan. The Wolverines would have opened the Brink's trucks. Instead, he decided to stay in the South for his chance to beat those hated Buckeyes.

He's a better people-person and a pretty good coach.

Fans will appreciate his dedication, his long-term commitment to the Tigers and, of course, the Ws. Miles' attitude is more fan-friendly. To fans of Tiger Nation, he looks like one of them. He wears a half cap and his emotions on his sleeve.

In the ensuing moments after Monday's win, BCS officials handed Miles a leather jacket to wear during the coronation ceremony. He shunned the gesture to wear the black jacket, instead wanting to proudly display his purple and gold colors.

"I'm LSU," Miles said repeatedly. He could even eventually, but it's not hard to see where his heart lies.

• See LANG 3C

INSIDE

Page 2C
LSU's Flynn, Jean-Francois named MVPs
How they scored, game stats

Page 3C
HEIST: Reliving a wild ride of a season
TOMPKINS: SEC's best rises again

Page 4C
Turnovers, penalties doom Buckeyes
ALLEN: Win was picture perfect enough

Page 5C
The Times' quarterly report: Check out how the game developed, quarter by quarter

Page 6C
A page of photos of the game, as seen by Times photographers in the Superdome.

RELATED COVERAGE
• A score-by-score review of the BCS national championship, 2C
• Go to thenewsstar.com for expanded coverage of the BCS national championship

---

SPORTS
SECTION C TUESDAY, January 8, 2008 The News-Star/thenewsstar.com

Prep hoops
Local prep teams face off as district play heats up
Details on 3C

LSU 38 | Ohio State 24

TITLE TIGERS
LSU wins second national championship in four years

ULM splits North Texas
Warhawk men lose, women win against Mean Green

By Mike Lapresti
Gannett News Service

NEW ORLEANS — In case you forgot about this point, LSU cleared up about Roger Clemens' legal file...

Quarterback Matt Flynn celebrates with Early Doucet after an LSU touchdown. Matt Flynn was named Offensive MVP of the BCS national championship game.

BOTTOM OF THE 1ST
Bateman finishes 23rd in Hawaii

Ohio State can't handle LSU

By Glenn Guilbeau

NEW ORLEANS — Can't See LSU? Can't Catch LSU. Can't Be LSU.

"And it sure feels good to win!

—James Carville